Tested Innocence

A MEMOIR

BERNADETTE JEUDY

DEDICATION

I dedicate my memoir to my beloved Chrystie.
You are the greatest joy of my life. Continue to push for
the stars. Always remember that happiness is a choice!

ACKNOWLEDGEMENTS

Thank you to Yvette R. Blair, my editor. I am thankful for you and your patience. Thank you for keeping my voice. You've made my thought process flow flawlessly. Thank you to Brandi Etheredge for designing such a beautiful book inside and out.

I would like to thank my friend, Theresa Powell (Teety), for spending tireless evenings, weekends, and vacation time to read and review my book. I am thankful that God has found a way to bring you back into my life, and I am particularly grateful for your friendship.

Thank you to my childhood friend, Darnie Tranquille (Dee), for taking the time to read and reread my memoir to ensure that every punctuation was in the right place, and for providing me with much-needed feedback from the perspective of a professional Haitian woman.

Thank you to my sister, Pascale (Patsy), for helping me remember, even though our version of the stories often differs. Thank you for your feedback and encouragement.

Thank you to my dearest friend, Marcia Hamilton (Anne), for always being there and for reading every excerpt that I've sent you. Your unselfish friendship has impacted my life in more ways than I could ever imagine. Thank you for becoming my extended family and for allowing me the honor to be the Godmother of my beautiful Taylor!

Thank you to my friends, Erline Cadichon and Carline Cadichon, for always encouraging me and making me believe that my story was worth publishing. Thank you for being kind and sweet and always consistent.

Thank you to my dearest cousin, Guilaine Wadopian (Guilou), who is always there, reading, rereading and encouraging me to push forward every day. I appreciate you for being you and being there in the most challenging moments of my life. You've seen me fall, rise, break down, and smile and yet you've always remained the sweetest and dearest Guilou.

Thank you to my friend, Estelle Jean (Dr. Jean), for taking time out of your busy schedule to read my excerpts and give me much needed feedback.

Thank you to my dearest sister, Lumine Damour, for always helping me put back the puzzle pieces of my life together.

Thanks to all my family and my circle of friends who have always been my biggest cheerleaders.

Lastly, thank you to the men who have loved me and to the ones that have walked away. I am a better human because of all of you!

CONTENTS

CHAPTER ONE

Unfulfilled Childhood Reflections

My mind was like a sailboat, taken to a quiet sea at night with anticipation that quietness could change at any moment. For the first time in a long time, I actually looked out of my window from the second floor of my split-level home in the small town of New Hempstead, New York. I could still see the full green leaves dancing to the sound of a warm spring evening. The sun was calm and peaceful, slowly dissipating behind the clouds as the nightfall made its way in. It was a joyous night, and for some strange reason, I was becoming aware of my surroundings while listening to the legendary Miles Davis – "I Fall in Love Too Easily." Come to think of it, I hadn't seen a star in a very long time. Was it because my curiosity for many things had been dormant, or was it because I deliberately shut my eyes to the beauty of nature? Perhaps I became indifferent to avoid feeling too vulnerable or facing my truth?

I had masterfully discarded most negative thoughts in my mind; however, my lack of awareness did not mean that I wasn't hurting, as I have cried in the dark a few times. Even now, my many "why" questions have remained unanswered. I was mostly in denial, and there was always a somber feeling that was painfully crushing my sense of normalcy; my forced moments of joy were sparse and devoid of meaning.

I forced myself to unconsciously enjoy every moment, as I reluctantly reminded myself that life is short and time lost worrying about things beyond my control is forever wasted. I've realized that time waits for no one, and it is undoubtedly one of the commodities that can't be bought.

As each year passed, I grew older, lacking the ability to detect the wisdom that is often associated with age. Most of the time, soulful songs were dancing in my mind, but laughter was seldom present. It seemed as though there was always a dark cloud standing in my way, and I couldn't help the worries that were haunting me, deep down in my soul. I always felt physically present and yet mentally, far away. I could never feel at home. Perhaps I needed to allow my mind to come up with the best possible scenarios and solutions that work for everyone else, but I always managed to exclude myself from the equation. I can't recall when, but somewhere along the way, I somehow learned to love myself.

I've had much time to reflect on my life and wondered what I could have done better to change the course, but it appears that merely learning from my experiences may not have been enough. The child within me was still longing for answers, and I wasn't sure how to reconcile with all these vivid memories that were rushing through my brain. Perhaps my cure was to let my bothered subconscious speak, but loudly this time. My hands trembled as I started writing the first few words.

Barefoot and free of worries, I remember walking on the beach not even feeling the slight discomfort of the hot white sand. In this hidden town of Gommier, built under the legend of Antoine Nan Gommier, southwest of Haiti, I ran, I played, and I ate grilled wild sardines with freshly made soft cassava topped with a delicious but slightly spicy sauce from the street vendors. As I saw the other children running away from the waves, I knew it was time to head home. I walked through the unpaved roads surrounded by beautiful majestic trees. I hopped and skipped. Everything was so alive! I had a broad smile as I picked up two ripe avocados under the avocado tree and two mangos from the adjacent tree right before I reached the hill.

As I continued my journey toward home on this beautiful afternoon, my little hands were not strong enough to hold all the avocados, and mangoes that I picked up along the way. Trying to juggle them against the stride of my pace, I lost my balance a few times, and my handful of harvest nearly freed itself from my embrace. Holding two of each of the delicious fruit, I discovered it was a lot to coordinate. Just before I reached home, the light storm washed my little soul with its intensity. These were the days I welcomed the cleanliness of the rain, and I was not afraid to dance under the mixture of rain and cloudy sun. My innocent five-year-old mind didn't care who was watching. My carefree stroll was interrupted as one of the avocados I gleefully collected fell out of my hands and smashed at my feet. It was time to get home to my Nana.

It must have been four in the afternoon when I nearly reached home. I noticed the sugar cane mill was still running. Two strong men were feeding the mill with sugar canes while the horses slowly moved in a circular motion to keep the loud motor going. Other workers were piling up the waste coming out of the mill into a chariot to perhaps later use for something else. I can't precisely recall how they transported all the juice from the sugar cane; however, I do remember a large container which boiled more than 120 degrees, with the help of woods and black charcoal. As I gazed from afar, the yellowish hot flames and the greyish smoke of the impressive hot syrup-making machine reminded me that I must get home for supper. I always admired the miracle of boiled sugar cane juice, turning into a thick syrup the next day. My great uncle, Leon, owned that mill, and he was the head of a vast extended family.

As I started running toward home, I briefly noticed Alicia, who was holding a young baby in her arms. Alicia was the former maid and current concubine to my uncle whom we'll refer to as "Jack." Concubines were quite common back then and were welcomed to live in the family home alongside the wives. On some rare occasions, the two adversaries laughed and talked together, but most of the time, the sense of disdain they shared between one another could not be mistaken. The worn frown lines of sadness were apparent in their faces, perhaps formed as they dreamt for another life, another world, or maybe, a man of their own.

I admired our small, modest house from a distance. It embodied such character as it stood on many acres of land right next to a tall coconut tree. It appeared to be quite content and thankful for the brief rainfall. The light wind made me appreciate the ripped yellow bananas stacked in between the greenest leaves I've ever seen, located right behind the house. I was tempted to grab a banana from the tree but was startled by the unmistakable blare of my Nana's voice calling me from afar. I froze in place, leaving behind the delicious banana to ripe another day.

As I approached the front porch, I was met with the heavenly smell of steamed fish, usually freshly caught from the nearby deep blue sea. Spinach from the wild garden was definitely on the menu, and my least favorite – boiled yams and plantains – neither of which were too pleasing to the palate. I pouted as I noticed the white residue of the dark charcoal used for our daily cooking. The aroma slowly escaped the grill, as the burnt charcoal engraved a permanent spot on the unfinished floor. It reminded me of the white sand from the beach. I marveled at how charcoal could be so dark yet turn into a sandy white powder.

My Nana, who was no more than five feet tall, loved me. She raised me until I was the age of five, along with my brothers and sister. Nana had the prettiest brown eyes and soft black hair with a few strands of grey. Her fine lines were gentle and added character to her light brown skin, which appeared to be darker due to the unforgiving 85-degree Haitian sunshine. My Nana was a quiet woman, she never raised her voice, and I never heard her laugh out loud, but she was one of the greatest storytellers around. Every night from what I remember, she would gather all her grandchildren on the big open porch. There we sat attentively, under the star-filled Caribbean sky listening to stories only worthy of a legend. At times she would sing during her stories, to better invoke the essence of her tale and allowed our imagination to travel through time.

Nana was not a woman of many words, except during storytelling time under the bright illuminated stars of Gommier. Electricity was scarce, so the yellow flames from the gas lamps, the full moon, and bright stars kept us company on many nights. Nana often allowed me and my sister to comb through her long soft hair. She would often take long walks near her garden, which was full of the greenest and sweetest vegetables. There was no such thing as genetically modified organisms in our little piece of heaven. She also liked to tour the large tobacco plantation. I imagine that it may have evoked fond memories of my grandfather. I never had the chance to meet him since he died before I was born. I believed that Nana missed him terribly, although she seldom spoke of him. She didn't smoke, but I remembered her distinctively chewing tobacco powder; I never could understand why, but Nana was unconventional, and her love for me was unmistakable.

Friday evening, the drum and the unison sound of "ayibobos" created an echo on top of the mountain, where my great aunt's small country house was located. The sound of the women's voices became louder as they chanted to the drumbeats. As the sound of tribal rhythms intensified, we knew it was time for Aunt Val's ritual voodoo ceremony. My brothers and I ran along toward that ancestral sound. My little sister was too young to tag along, so we left her behind. As we got closer, we hid behind the vetiver plantation. The ritual had begun! There, we saw mostly women in white dresses, hair wrapped with white or red bandanas, as they all lined up in a perfect circle. They were dancing and chanting to the rigorous drum, led by a shirtless man with a round belly, as droplets of sweat rolled down their stoic faces. We patiently waited and doltishly laughed silently out of sight, behind the vetiver field.

The drummer appeared to be already drunk as the pure white 80% proof bottle of alcohol was strategically placed right next to him. The women's expressions were severe. No smiles were visible. I wondered how their actions could contradict so much with their emotions. I noticed Aunt Val in all white clothing sitting in the middle of the circle speaking in a non-familiar dialect. She raised her hands toward the grey sky as to give a signal. It was time to serve food to their 'gods'. There was a lot of food, mostly meat from perhaps a goat, a cow and dozens of chickens that took their last breath earlier that day. Children were forbidden to participate, but we were always fascinated by this ritual from a distance. Suddenly the chants were getting louder and closer as they were surprisingly approaching the vetiver plantation. My heart skipped a beat; frozen in fear, we couldn't run. Silence was golden at that moment, but we couldn't stop laughing as our young minds outsmarted those foolish adults. I've lost count of how many voodoo ceremonies my siblings, cousins, and I have witnessed. But every time, one of us would whisper, "does Aunt Val really think the spirits are eating the foods?" I guess that this was one of the reasons me and my siblings never believed that the "spirits" existed, but rather a creation of my great aunt's imagination. Aunt Val's voodoo ceremonies became an entertaining experience, rather than a spiritual one. Besides, Nana was very religious, and she never expressed an opinion of her sister's beliefs.

Two women were holding the trays of food followed by the rest of the partisans. They stopped ceremoniously right before they reached the plantation. My aunt gave orders to start serving the food by throwing each piece of meat in an orderly fashion into the opposite direction of the vetiver plantation. By then we were joined by several other cousins, but still hiding quietly. We caught and devoured almost every single piece of chicken or goat, or whatever came in our direction. I curiously wondered whether my aunt thought the gods really ate the food. We laughed and ran back to Nana's house just in time for nighttime stories.

The aroma of the morning coffee awakened my senses as I made my way to my Aunt Gracie's house for breakfast the next morning. She barely smiled, as her subtle beauty was hidden behind her premature fine lines and sad brown eyes. Aunt Gracie had four children, three of them bore her last name, which was a common theme amongst Nana's children. Aunt Gracie lived with her partner, an un-divorced man, and father of one of her children. I gathered that most women in my family were broken souls. They were nurturing and often enabled unaccept-able dalliances from men. It was common for men to have a wife and multiple concubines with several children outside of their "marriage." The wives were often the ones who picked up the broken pieces and stepped up to raise their husbands' fatherless children. Their unspoken secrets could have communicated a thousand thoughts to the world.

My Aunt Gracie never mentioned a word to my cousins about their father, and there was an unspoken understanding. Their hearts may have wondered a few times, but they probably never dared to question their mother. Perhaps Aunt Gracie was replicating the legacy of mul-tiple children with different last names. The thought of not knowing whether their father was dead or alive must have surely haunted their minds. In our family, certain things were better left unsaid and buried forever. For what it's worth, I heard I had a father... It was a culture of complacency, uncomfortable tolerance, and laissez-faire comportment. I have watched my aunt's oldest daughter follow the same path with thirteen children on her own. Life happened in that unordinary little town. I observed, I learned, and I absorbed thoughts unconsciously.

Every Thursday morning, religiously, the short-bearded man with what appeared to be a doctor's suitcase, would show up. He was not a medical doctor, but a self-taught natural 'doctor.' I cringed every time he pulled out the small calabash container and the ugly black leeches that would soon be taking a temporary spot on my Nana's legs to suck her blood. He sat there for hours watching the leeches, perhaps slowly sucking the life out of her. She suffered from inflammation, and I guess that was his way of attempting to treat her disease. Nana stopped walking as the pain became so severe, and her health quickly declined. She must have had diabetes and didn't even know it. The legendary fairy tales under the star-filled sky ceased the night Nana died, and so did my innocence.

I felt pain but was too young to understand the impact that losing her had on my life. The change was rather sudden and entirely unexpected, as are most things in life. When I sat still long enough and allowed my thoughts to vanish through the sound of unsung classical religious songs, I could hear my Nana's voice reassuring me to embrace life with my chin up and to smile brightly at my new world with courage. "March on Dety, march on," Nana's voice repeated. I believed her encouraging words, and I slowly marched on to embrace my new life with a hint of hesitation.

CHAPTER TWO

My Subconscious Thoughts

My chest tightened, and I wanted to cry as I said my last goodbye to the sandy beach, the bluest sea, and the sweetest mangos and bananas when my beautiful Nana passed. As I remembered it, in my five-year-old mind, the desynchronized squawk of the roosters woke me up at three in the morning. I was pensive as I heard the dogs cry louder than usual that Saturday. How I wished I petted them; they were always our faithful protectors. I loved them from a distance, and I knew I would miss them, especially Lapolice. He must have known I was leaving my nest and venturing to the unknown world as he came a little closer toward me; his silence and long stare were powerful.

The wild chickens made an appearance; I opted not to feed them their natural dried corn that morning as my detachment was inevitable. I listened to their clucks with amazement, as if it were for the first time. The tree leaves danced through the shadow as my Uncle Leon saddled the horses. It was as if each uniquely engraved leaf waved for my attention, in a bid to wish me farewell.

The streets of Gommier were vacant as the horses made their way to the Wharf Jeremie. I was on one horse with my Uncle Leon, and my siblings were on the other three horses along with other family members. I could not see anything along the road as it was still dark, but I welcomed the fresh non-polluted air. I told my uncle that my butt was hurting, and the ride was quite uncomfortable, but he ignored me. My Aunt Gracie must have braided my two cornrows too tight as I felt a slight pound in my temple. I became restless, and my uncle held me tight to protect me from falling off the horse. I heard the sounds of the other horses right behind me, and I was unknowingly thankful for having been raised by an entire village.

Saturday morning, I fought back my tears as I reluctantly boarded the intimidating and dangerous Anne-Marie Florida. The overcrowded 150-foot ferry, with three decks full of different types of merchandise, appeared gigantic to my five-year-old eyes. Traveling by ferries during that time was the most affordable means of transportation between Jeremie and Port-au-Prince. My siblings and I were accompanied by Victoria, my godmother, who was headed to Port-au-Prince to sell goods for the upcoming school year. I held on tight to Victoria's hands throughout the ride as I was getting seasick. The merchants were anxious and couldn't wait to perhaps unload and sell their merchandise. I noticed most of the passengers on the ferry were women, and most of them had permanent frown lines on their forehead. My siblings and I were agitated and quite scared of the vast sea.

I contemplated the deep blue sea with a curious eye, and its authority was powerful. The droplets of the hard rain made it seem so much more terrifying. The mighty wind made its presence felt, as the daylight was peeking, and the clouds conspired to ensure the usual bright sunshine stayed out of sight. The boat was moving at an unprecedented speed, and I felt scared. Suddenly the voices of the passengers became somewhat louder, and I noticed my little feet were getting wet. Victoria screamed as the slim woman next to us hugged her child closer to her heart. She appeared to be trembling, and she didn't say a word. She was probably praying throughout the whole twelve-hour ride, wondering whether that day was her last. I didn't quite understand the seriousness of the situation, but I was fearful as everyone was either crying or praying. I suddenly realized that our ferry was being swallowed by the audacious body of blue water and was slowly sinking with over 790 passengers.

My siblings and I panicked, and we started to cry. We felt trapped as there was no emergency plan in place. Several vessels had sunk underwater during that year, and many people never had the chance to say goodbye to their loved ones. The prospect of getting out of Anne-Marie Florida alive that day was slim to none. By some miracle, we arrived on the National Port of Port-au-Prince to see another day. Another life was in plain sight, and God surely had other plans for me.

I officially started to make acquaintance with my mother, who came to collect her four children from the National Port of Port-au-Prince. I barely knew her as she left for the States when I was very young. She appeared to be very strict and unapproachable. She was slim, petite, and quite beautiful; her deep brown complexion was very much similar to mine. I knew I wouldn't forget her face this time. I barely looked at her during Nana's funeral, but I was somewhat curious to get to know her. I looked at her swollen red eyes full of tears and realized she was still dealing with the loss of her mother, my Nana, who died too soon at the age of 60.

I sympathized with her, and I thought maybe she wasn't so bad and perhaps she could possibly love me as Nana did. I walked toward her and stood still right next to her. I wanted to hug her but restrained myself. I never realized that she had long arms, until she pulled all four of us closer, and hugged us tightly. This was one of the rare times my mother hugged me.

She attempted to say a few words in a broken sentence. "Everything…is…going to be ok. Everything…."

It was difficult for her to speak, and even at a young age, I could feel her pain.

"Be Ok." My little sister, Patsy, repeated the words as she clung to my mother. Hody followed with assurance. "Be ok, mom." I just allowed my tears to flow and remained silent throughout the bumpy ride to our new home. It appeared that my siblings and I learned at a young age how to deal with our pain in silence. Sometimes no words were necessary.

We settled in Rue de La Reunion in a gated five-bedroom house. Life was entirely different than in the countryside. Food was not as abundant and not as readily accessible. There were very few fruit trees in sight. I came to the realization that nothing was for free as my mother had to purchase everything, even sugar cane, which we had in abundance in Gommier.

My sister, Patsy, and I shared a bedroom, but often, I slept alone since my sister spent most of her time sick and hospitalized for months. Patsy was two years younger than me, and we almost shared the same birth date. She was born on February 25, and my birthdate is on February 26. I always found this fact fascinating and never understood how my mom managed to give birth to two girls two years apart, yet on almost the same day of the month. My sister always resented sharing her special day with me, and she never enjoyed her birthday, while I subconsciously and selfishly wanted to be the center of attention. I noticed that her complexion was about a shade lighter than mine; I always wondered if this was because she had a different father than me. Her thick long hair was very much like mine, but the shape of her beautiful face was much rounder than my elongated bone structure. My sister suffered from severe bronchitis and often had uncontrollable asthma attacks. She was away from home most of the time, and at one point, I thought that she lived in the hospital. I never really had a chance to bond with my little sister, as she was either fighting to stay alive or away at a boarding school.

Initially, my mother had enough money to sustain the monthly rent, food, and a maid to take care of us. This transition was a significant change for me, and I assumed for my siblings as well. The evening stars were replaced by electrical lights, and they were mostly out of sight except on some rare nights. I often welcomed the occasional blackout just to peek at a star that seemed so small and so far out of reach in comparison to Gommier's. The rain wasn't as clean here; in fact, I caught a cold for attempting to play in the rain in my backyard. The musky rainwater took a permanent spot in our enclosed, small unfinished patio. There was nowhere to run or dance freely. The four rectangular walls framing our yard always seemed like they were closing in on me as I tried to twirl like a ballerina. The dirty puddle of water that simply sat in my yard due to lack of drainage splashed on my face as I attempted to jump up and down.

"Help!" I closed my eyes and screamed.

My brother, Joe, rushed toward me and removed me from the rain.

"One of these days, you are going to hit your head on these walls." As he carried me, his voice was stern.

"I think I have mud in my eyes."

Joe looked at me, first gazing at my right eye. His caramel brown eyes glistened.

"Stop shutting your eyes. If there's mud in them, your eyes will be sealed."

Joe was doing what big brothers do – using this moment at my expense for fun and games.

"That's not going to happen." At least I hoped it wasn't true. I kept my eyes open for as long as I could without blinking.

"You're getting water all over the floor." Joe looked at the mess I had made. I grabbed some towels from our kitchen and gathered up all the water.

I became melancholy, but I felt that I needed to let go of certain things, even though I didn't quite understand most of my feelings. Interestingly, my siblings never liked to play in the rain, but they always watched me run in a circle through our opened back door leading to the small patio. The clean, crisp, and refreshing free-flowing water that I used to love became an annoyance rather than a form of enjoyment, as my stuffy nose warned me to stay out of the unfriendly rain next time.

My kindergarten class was a welcome addition to my new life. I was required to wear the cutest pink striped uniform, that my mother had to purchase from the school. I was also delighted with my matching hair barrettes; I thought I always had a flair for fashion. I played freely with other kids in the schoolyard, and I noticed the two little girls who lived in the house next to ours. One of them said, "you are my new neighbor and my new friend!" I nodded and smiled. My mother never allowed me and my siblings to play with our neighbor's kids; therefore, the school became a happy place, as I had the freedom to play with whomever I wanted to during our long recess hour. I felt like I knew everyone in my kindergarten class, but I never made any friends. I felt my mother wouldn't approve of my new friends, but I took comfort knowing that I could always run, dance, and play in school. My mother kept us sheltered and overprotected. For the first few months, we lived with my mother. She didn't work as she had just returned from the States, and was patiently awaiting our green cards. My mother's hope faded the day she was denied re-entry to the States.

The intricacies of life during my mother's ten-year period of living back in Haiti had taught her resilience. She learned to survive in a place where opportunities were lacking, and jobs were scarce. My siblings and I became closer and quickly learned how to protect each other. My mother, a former teacher, instilled in us that education was as necessary as food. She always found a way for us to acquire the best knowledge that we could. The girls went to an all-girls school, and my brothers attended an all-boys school. My mom had a vision for us and made every sacrifice to shape that vision.

We remained sheltered living in our own world that mom created for us. We did not have much, but we never had time to ponder on this sad reality as we were always busy and surrounded by people who had more, except the time when Clo reminded me of my demise. Through my many curricular activities, I met many acquaintances who were from wealthy families. Since I was at the top of my class, I received some awards and scholarships, one of which was for music. Music lessons took place on Friday after school, and I always felt proud carrying the small black leather case containing my loaner black clarinet with the shiny silver keys. As I walked into the large room, the baby grand piano took center stage and commanded my attention. Mrs. Belle, the music teacher, always stood unwelcomingly in the middle of the room facing the entrance door. Her skin was a very light complexion, and I always thought she was white until I heard her speak, on a rare occasion, in perfect Haitian Creole. Each girl quickly took her place in front of the music stand that held multiple music sheets. She never smiled, and I found her to be very strict and unfriendly. I still vividly remember her monotone voice, "I hope you practiced. I want to hear one unison sound. Do you understand?" I heard she was a classically trained musician from some known university in the United States. There were six other girls in the class who resembled Mrs. Belle. I immediately noticed their light-skinned complexion compared to my dark chocolate skin. They mostly kept to themselves except when we attempted to play a musical piece together. At first, I was excited until I started feeling lonely, discouraged, and I realized that the soothing and intriguing sound that I often admired through French jazz music required an insane amount of practice. I only managed to make unpleasant sounds with the clarinet and the trombone - never to become good at either.

I even received a scholarship for an electronic course on the weekends. Every Saturday morning, I was forced to wake up early and I walked a few blocks to board the crowded Taptap heading to Delmas 48. I still felt sleepy and tired by the time I arrived in class. This was supposed to be a six-month course, and I had already imagined the end of the course on my second day. The small non-ventilated room was hot and humid. There were about fifteen of us in the class. The other boys and girls seemed to be curious and had a genuine interest in exploring what lies beyond a light bulb. I, on the other hand, was thinking about the volleyball game I was missing. I remember Mr. Michel yelling across the room, "Jeudy, are you with us today?" Who in their right mind would give me a scholarship for electronics?! I grew disinterested, so I allowed my brother, Hody, to take over the assignment portion of the course. Frankly, this scholarship would have been more fitting for Hody as he used to build radios from scratch and was fascinated by anything electronics. He welcomed the opportunity to practice what he probably already knew through his young genius mind and imagination.

My family usually visited Patsy at St. Madeleine's School, an all-girls boarding school, every first Sunday of the month. One particular Sunday, I heard on the radio about the rise of some political turmoil; because of this news, the sisters of St. Madeleine felt that it was best to send everyone home, as the teachers couldn't make it to the school. Patsy was the only person that didn't get picked up that day. Honestly, I don't think Patsy ever liked being in boarding school, but this wasn't a choice she could make. She became accustomed to being away from home and her family most of her life. She often said, "I just got dumped at St. Madeleine." Secretly I think she resented my mother for it. I went to pick her up the next day after volleyball practice. As I got off the Taptap three blocks away from St. Madeleine, I saw a large crowd protesting, perhaps against hunger or lack of jobs. Dictatorships and failed presidencies, road closures and burning of tires became the norm on the unstable island of Haiti. Perhaps that is why I've never liked big crowds and protests. I could feel every heavy beat of my heart. I became anxious and frightened as I heard the sounds of gunshots not too far from me. My athletic legs became stronger as I ran as fast as I could through the dusty streets of downtown to avoid getting accidentally killed. As I ran for my life, I felt grateful that my volleyball coach pushed me. My legs were strong and may have possibly saved my life that day.

I could see the massive brown gates off into the distance as I slowly approached the intimidating fortress with much trepidation. The skinny guard looked me over and summoned me to follow him toward the main building. Wonderfully tangled grapevines dangled from the sky, creating cascades of shade along the walkway; a welcomed distraction from the rather unfriendly security guard walking just ahead of me. I could tell that the grapes hanging from the vines were ripe and sweet, but I was afraid to reach out and grab the low hanging fruit that almost touched my forehead. The benches on the side of the entrance were adorned with several species of roses and enclosed by a beautiful gated garden. There was a sense of serenity that made me feel at peace. The silence that absorbed me as I walked toward the main building was a stark difference from the bustling sounds of downtown.

Sister Yvonne, wearing her blue robe, high white collar, and white veil cascading over her back, firmly greeted me. She half smiled and said, "Patsy has been waiting since yesterday. Tell your mother to make sure she picks her up on time the next time." Then she vanished through a long dark corridor to collect Patsy, as I waited in the sizeable mysterious waiting room with penetrating sunlight through the large cleaned glass windows. A few minutes later, Patsy appeared with her oversized loopy glasses, her tiny brown suitcase, and exclaimed, "Finally!"

My mother always wanted me to attend St. Madeleine, but fortunately, I was not accepted due to the age restrictions. My mother pleaded with the sisters to waive their requirements, but Catholic schools were known to be very strict on not bending their rules. I was relieved when I received my rejection letter. I smiled from the inside and must have done 15 handstand flips in my mind. My vivid imagination was wild, and I wanted to explore the world from the outside, not from behind the massive gates of strict nuns, full of frustration due to sex deprivation. On our way home, I was lost in my thoughts and imagined being in another place riding on a clean bus along a road full of green trees.

One day, I saw my mother cry for the first time when she was desperately trying to fix her only comfortable pair of shoes. She started working at a factory and still couldn't earn enough money for necessary living expenses. She lost her financial stability as well as her sense of pride. I saw her sitting in the kitchen on a small bench as she broke down. I did not move, nor did I have the words to say. I quietly went back to bed; perhaps this was the day she realized she had to care for four children on her own with no stable income. I started to understand that every strong woman has a breaking point. It was then that I realized that my new life was going to be quite different than how I imagined it in my mind. I noticed that I was in an environment that stopped me from seeing the beauty and all the wonders of nature. As I was reaching the world of adolescence, I started to reflect a bit more on my early childhood, and I began to understand and see all the imperfections of the vast Lebrun Plantation in Gommier.

I found the concubinage culture immoral and repulsive. I developed undirected anger toward all the men and women in my family who had allowed this senseless behavior to continue. I'd begun to understand that Alicia did not choose the life of a mistress; she was raped, and her circumstances became her reality. She couldn't provide financially for herself and her child, and with nowhere to run, she succumbed to her circumstances. It turns out, Gommier was what I imagined it would be... in a fairytale. Perhaps I was living through Nana's vivid tales under the stars. Unfortunately, Gommier was no fairytale... I know this now.

The hidden secrets and immoral values were slowly sucking the natural beauty out of my native town. I'd become detached, perhaps traumatized. Even the memories of the sweetest coconut water, mangos, and sugar cane couldn't make up for my discontentment. Gommier was no longer my home, and I no longer felt a connection to the town I once cherished. I realized the day my Nana died, Gommier had stopped being my home. I wondered how many untold stories Nana had to take to her grave. My memories of her and her unconditional love were slowly becoming a blur.

My mother downgraded to a one-room studio apartment in Rue Chavannes, Port-au-Prince, which became my permanent home, where I would grow up with my sister and two brothers. Mom was rarely home as she was the breadwinner of the family, and her daily commute via the colorful Taptaps was quite long, leaving my older brother Joe, who was a child himself, to care for us. I never liked the dynamic between my mom and my older brother; there was always friction. The unspoken pain hung over our household like a dark cloud. There were brief, unexpected explosions of feelings, and exchanges of meaningless words. One day, I overheard my mother say to my brother Joe, "I put a curse on you." My mother's words and expression never left my mind. I remember my brother, very slim and much taller than my mother, standing there motionless for at least thirty seconds, and I couldn't read his thoughts nor his emotions, as he remained silent and simply looked at my mother before he abruptly walked away. I knew my mother didn't mean what she said, but I couldn't help but wonder whether my brother's life would have turned out differently had my mother never uttered those words. I should have learned that day that words had a funny way of manifesting themselves.

My mother was dealing with her own demons and punishing us for inconsequential noncompliance; perhaps the only way for her to release her frustration. She entered the United States with a visa around 1978, and like many others, she overstayed her welcome. A few years later, she was finally qualified for a green card through her brother, who was a naturalized U.S. citizen. The catch was that she had to return to Port-au-Prince to obtain her green card from the U.S. Embassy. She was excited that she was finally coming out of the shadows of illegal immigration, but unfortunately, she chose the wrong time to have a disagreement with her brother. He held the financial power and declined to sponsor her immigration application as initially planned. In a letter to my mother, my uncle, an excellent writer, quoted a Bible verse, "You are dust, and to dust, you shall return." I never understood what he meant then, but my mother often repeated those words until they became a powerful reminder for her. My mother was crushed. She had to become reacquainted with the new reality of living back in Haiti as a single mother of four fatherless children. Her constant state of melancholy revealed her struggles and disappointment.

Rue Chavannes was a small community with a long corridor that led to three different houses. Our studio apartment was in the very first house that we shared with another family. We barely interacted with them. There was another small blue house adjacent to ours, where the neighbor, Clo, lived with her two nephews and her niece. Her house became our permanent spot on Thursday nights to watch Haitian comedy on her black and white television. We did not have a TV at home, but we were encouraged by my mother to read countless books. And finally, the last house belonged to the landlord and his family. My very first best friend, Manou, was his youngest daughter. Our landlord operated his appliance repair shop there, and the early morning lively conversations among the workers became my 6:00 AM alarm clock. Broken refrigerators were permanent fixtures throughout the small community.

Growing up under the Baby Doc regime made me quickly understand at a young age to stay out of political conversations. Finding a hobby was the best way to keep out of trouble under an oppressive regime. School, reading, and volleyball became my passions. I couldn't quite recall how I've acquired so many books as money was scarce, but my sister and I read hundreds of books. My friend Manou joined the same volleyball club, and we had practice four days a week. Our coach, Fanfan, pushed us to recognize our ability to reach new heights every day. The 100 squats punishment imposed by my coach for careless mistakes made me stronger. I became a stronger athlete, and the volley court at College St. Pierre became my favorite place in the world. We spent a lot of time together listening to French jazz songs; we often stopped and rewound the cassette tapes to write down the lyrics of our favorite songs. Manou was about my age and was hilariously funny. "Dety, are you ready to squash them with your powerful serve?" as she inquired as she referred to an upcoming volleyball game. Manou was slim and much taller than me. Her two French braids became her signature hairstyle, and her dark chocolate skin always seemed more beautiful in the sun as she spiked the ball and crushed one of the opponents. We also started to branch out to listening to Haitian music as Emeline Michel became more popular, and I was often told that I looked like her. My early teenage years were made up of romantic stories from Harlequin romance novels and French monthly romance magazines. My interest in boys started to be at the forefront of my mind when I became fifteen. I started spending a lot of time with Dany, the boy next door, one of Clo's nephews.

It was November 25, around 6:00 PM, that Dany and I were alone and ignoring the sound of the television in the background; we engaged in an intense and rather exciting conversation. I was becoming acutely aware of certain unusual feelings that I felt toward him. Dany's intelligence and kindness drew me to him. There was one question that brought clarity to our hidden feelings for each other. I remember asking him if his girlfriend was coming to see him since it was his birthday, and he replied that he did not have a girlfriend.

I asked him, "What about Judith?" As he looked at me with a rather serious gaze, he said something along the line, "If she were my girlfriend, she would have been here with me."

I found a sense of comfort and attachment when I was around Dany. His attentiveness toward me magnetized my curiosity.

Dany was a few years older than me and appeared to be much more mature than I was. From that evening, to deter the vigilance of his Aunt Clo, we continued our secret conversations by way of subliminal notes. We allowed our thoughts to flow freely through written words, without being too direct or open about our feelings, our primitive form of texting, I guess.

He asked a lot of questions, "What is your favorite color? Who's your favorite artist, and how do you see me?" This was his way of getting a little deeper into my world.

I was somewhat mysterious, and often diverted a question that I deemed challenging to answer. I could not hold back my emotions when Dany openly confessed his love for me on his birthday. "I will always have a burning desire to protect you and fight for you. Know that your beautiful smile brightens my day, my forever love," he said. I was afraid, somewhat excited, and ironically confused. I left his house without a word. Although I secretly liked him, I wasn't sure what to do nor ready to embark in the premature journey of intimate love. I went back to his house thirty minutes later to explain that I was too young, and I wanted to focus on my studies. I concluded with, "I hope you understand where I am coming from Dany." Was I playing hard to get?

I could not sense whether Dany felt disoriented or embarrassed, but he apologized for having offended me. The next day, I dramatically told him that I loved him by way of a short love letter: "My heart beating faster every time I am around you is not a coincidence. I supposed I've always loved you, and I am sorry if I made you feel otherwise yesterday. I love you. Your Dety." He spent the whole day without opening the letter for fear of rejection. I could not focus during school and volleyball practice that day. My own fear of rejection was beginning to manifest itself and became increasingly intolerable. It took Dany two days to talk to me, and my heart breathed a sigh of relief when I read his words. He loved me, and I made it clear to him that our relationship should remain a secret, as I didn't want my mom or his aunt to find out. I was an audacious teenager.

On December 24, Clo suspected my relationship with Dany, when she found us in her house alone talking in the dark. She was clearly unsettled and said hurtful words that stung my heart like a bee.

"You are a little whore. You have nothing to offer. You actually think you can be with my nephew. Over my dead body." She spoke with fury in her eyes and anger in her voice.

I immediately exited her house. I noticed her stocky body, and she was a few pounds overweight as her frame appeared to be quite large for her 4'7" height. The gap between her stained yellow teeth seemed much more prominent than usual. She must have been in her late forties but looked much older as her hair was completely grey. The sweat dripping from her forehead made her fine lines more pronounced. Clo did not have a husband or boyfriend. Her nephews and niece were all she had. She probably felt that I was taking away one of her prized possessions, and in turn, became defensive. Clo reminded me that I was not good enough because of my financial circumstances. She did not mince any words, and the hurt stayed with me for a long time. My teary eyes expressed my sadness, anger, and disappointment; yet my sense of respect for elders prevented me from mustering a word.

My mother also found out at the same time as her ears could not escape the rather unpleasant words of Clo. Although mom was disappointed, she immediately shielded me with her protection. That was the first time that my heart allowed me to recognize that my mom loved me. My mother came out of our kitchen and gently placed her two loving hands on my shoulders while I was standing in front of our apartment. I was now directly in front of her, shaking with fear, as we walked closer to Clo's house. She briefly looked at me, then turned toward Clo to meet her eyes. She gestured her right hand toward my face, as her left hand was still comfortably resting on my shoulder.

She said to Clo with conviction in her voice: "Take a good look at my beautiful daughter. Take a good look at her. If I were to look for a man for her, I would go to Laboule, Turjeau, and Lalue. I wouldn't come to the slums where you and your nephew belong."

I was speechless and deep down, I felt terrible for Dany as those words were hurtful. I was forbidden to go to Clo's house and was reprimanded by my mother behind closed doors, and as a result, Dany and I began our one-year courtship with secret love letters. I grew up in a place where playing hard to get was the norm for young girls, and courtship was a necessary step to any romantic relationship. It was fascinating how much Dany and I loved each other. Our love was pure and innocent with no ulterior motive, and we never once attempted to have sexual relations.

We were always under the watchful eyes of adults, and so, we were hardly alone. Our intimacy consisted of a brief tender touch or a stolen kiss on rare occasions when I would convince my sister when she was home for vacation from boarding school to visit the beautiful park of Champs de Mars to get ice cream so that I could see Dany. I would also coordinate a rendezvous with him, as this was the only time we could freely see each other. Our story was simply a display of love between a boy and a girl. The flowers that he picked up by the roadside reinforced his love and reminded me that he was never far away. I sometimes wondered if I was actually in love with Dany; after all, I was barely a teenager, and I didn't quite understand the different emotions associated with love. Honestly, my understanding of love was solely inspired by French Harlequin romance novels. I associated love with romance, passion, and a never-ending fairy tale, where the girl always ends up happy with the handsome, rich man. I didn't understand the reality of love being like a boat at sea, docking at ports a few times, but still wandering for its final destination.

Growing up, my young heart started experiencing the rollercoaster of life, and my interests slowly gravitated toward boys outside of my small community. I remember when I was a child, Nana's love always had a way of healing my wounds. I knew then, with absolute certainty no matter how dark it got, the sun was just around the corner.

As a teenager, my mind started to gradually shift toward an unclear path. My self-assuredness began to diminish, slowly replaced with insecurity and despair. I became more dependent on other people for my happiness and began to seek attention from the world. I noticed that a youthful infatuation with my French teacher, Bau, began to take shape. He must have been in his late twenties and was quite charming; I was in over my head.

I soon noticed that all the girls in my class shared the same sentiments. Bau was charismatic, brilliant, and well spoken. He invited a few of his top students to his first book release, and like many other girls in my school, I wanted my crush to turn into something more. I wanted to be his chosen favorite. He was poetic and appeared to be successful. When I read his book for the fourth time, I started to develop a relationship with his writing. I began to express my thoughts on paper, and I began writing a novel based on my fictional father. I asked Bau to help me edit my pages to spend more quality time alone with him in his apartment. I enjoyed being so close to him and having unlimited access to him during my two-hour editing session every Sunday afternoon.

Interestingly, he never crossed the lines—although he was a little flirtatious at times, and his smile always made me feel special. I was fascinated by him. The way he spoke was somewhat poetic, and I wanted to be around him all the time. He was about 5'10", and his smile was magnetic and intoxicating; his soft light brown skin and medium built physique looked impeccable in his tailored pants and shirt. His debonair demeanor didn't go unnoticed. His husky and modulated voice sounded like it belonged on a radio or television show: "Now, I have full confidence that you all have read the assigned chapter. Let's begin." He would say this at the beginning of the class. Beau became what I desired, but he was so far out of my reach. Besides, every other girl wanted to have access to him.

One day, Dany followed me as he suspected that I was not going to volleyball practice as I had told my mother. My smile immediately faded when I spotted him as I was coming out of Bau's apartment. I wasn't sure how long he was waiting, nor did I ask him. He looked at me with disappointment in his watery eyes, and forcefully said, "You've deceived me, and I trusted you." His voice was hoarse, and his eyes were sad as he continued, "Do you know how much I love you?" He paused. "I can't be with you anymore. It's over between us." I couldn't say a word. Dany still walked me home, perhaps hoping for a reaction from me, but the unspoken silence said it all, *"You've messed up Dety."*

I did not look at him, nor did I attempt to defend myself. He was hurt and felt betrayed; he was heartbroken and rightfully so, as my intentions were not pure. Had Bau expressed a desire to be with me then, I would have gladly complied with his request. Dany broke up with me that day. My newly developed sense of pride wouldn't allow me to fight for him. He later told me that he experienced true love with me and that the end of our relationship remained a constant wound in his heart. I loved him in my own way, and the best way I knew how. Our love was convenient, and I liked that. As my mind was trying to figure out the next phase of my life, the love letters that I exchanged with Dany became a form of entertainment for my younger sister and her friends who were away at boarding school; their entertainment was at my expense. She deliberately took my letters from the box that I carefully placed under my bed, out of site.

My friendship and infatuation with Bau continued to blossom, especially when he was about to leave Haiti to migrate to the States. There was no exact science when it became love. I realized that it could happen at any time when you least expect it. The warm sunshine of Haiti was always present throughout the whole year, even during rainy days. I had only read about the four different seasons of the year in school books and novels but had yet to experience this wonder of nature. Ever since I could remember, I always craved the idea of having a father. Although my brother Hody's father loved me and even punished me because I refused to call him "dad," I could never accept him as my father. His name was Christophe, and he visited us almost every day, but I can't recall whether he was still romantically involved with my mother. I never saw my mother and him holding hands, or kiss affectionately. He was tall, and he was a handsome man, but I knew he wasn't my father, although his almost straight nose looked very much similar to mine. I wanted and needed my own father. I didn't even know where my father lived or what he looked like; yet the desire to meet him increased, especially after Dany broke up with me.

I refused to relinquish the thought that my father did not love me or did not want to see me. For years, I held on to the idea that I had my own dad. My hope of meeting him never dwindled, and ironically, I was never mad at him for not being present. I secretly blamed my

mother for keeping me away from him. I had silently wished for my father's presence on several occasions. While trying to mend my disconcerted heart, I was often upset with my mother for reasons that didn't quite make sense. Perhaps I was a bit rebellious, and it was easier to be mad at the person closest to me. There was one particular Sunday afternoon I became increasingly sad, and I just couldn't remain silent. I was frustrated, although I couldn't pinpoint the specific reason. A form of punishment that was often used by mother was for me to kneel on the concrete floor for what seemed to be a very long time. While my face was making acquaintance with the bare blue wall, I said to my mother in an angry tone, "I wish my father were here." I must have struck a chord and hurt my mother's feelings by uttering those words as I felt the heavy weight of her leather belt in my flesh. I screamed loudly. The day that my mother beat me for desiring my father was when I fully realized that I was indeed a fatherless child.

CHAPTER THREE

Hello New York

After a decade of struggles, my mother and her brother finally got tired of their juvenile disagreement and decided to resolve their differences. Once again, my uncle agreed to help my mother to migrate to the United States; this time legally. My mother traveled with my brother Hody, and left me, my sister, and my oldest brother, Joe, behind with our uncle, Lau. My sister, Patsy, and I were granted an immigration visa two years later, and Joe was still patiently waiting to join us. We had been preparing for the journey to America for about ten years. When the cockpit door was closed, we passed on our seatbelts, and the plane rolled on the tarmac and lifted into the air and took off. Silently, I said, *"Finally."* I was finally on my way to America; I was so lost in my thoughts and was overcome with joy and emotions that I wasn't even scared or nervous about my very first plane ride.

I entered the land of George Washington on a cold winter day in the year of 1990. The cloudy sky grimaced to announce the arrival of the white snow. As the plane descended, I saw thousands of colorful lights appearing from the horizon. Through the clouds, I caught a glimpse of many well-designed structured buildings, standing tall, and proudly welcoming me to my new life. I was amazed by all these wonders and never imagined a world as beautiful. As I exited the plane, the cold winter breeze informed me that I was underdressed with my fitted blue jeans, oversized short sleeve shirt, and open toe sandals. I was not quite ready for the treacherous and unforgiving winter. I knew then that I would surely miss the hot sunshine of my homeland.

Dr. Blot, my mother's friend and chaperone escorted my siblings and me to the immigration office with our large yellow envelopes containing our temporary green cards. I noticed a few people carrying a case of Rhum Barbancourt, the alcoholic beverage choice in Haiti. For some, Rhum Barbancourt would be the final reminder of their soon to be forgotten homeland as they would intend to never return. For others, it was perhaps a way to stay close to home or to keep them warm during the frigid winters in New York.

We arrived at Dr. Blot's home in Brooklyn, late in the night at 10:45. When I woke up the next day, I noticed a piece of cardboard and a small empty bag close to the sidewalk. I began to realize that the streets were not as spotless as I had always pictured in my mind. The same day, my mother collected us as the majestic George Washington Bridge stood still, and we crossed the vast Hudson River. I must admit that I was frightened as I saw myself getting closer to the grey sky, yet at the same time, I felt that I was on top of the world. I had a clear view of the illuminated city of Manhattan. It appeared that the Big Apple was always smiling and dancing at the same time. The multitude of lights sparked a sense of hope within me.

We drove along the Palisades Interstate Parkway. It was a fantastic site to see all the leafless trees, covered with white snow. The Parkway was dark, and the headlights of the Toyota Camry took us to our final destination. We arrived in our one-bedroom apartment, which wasn't particularly impressive. The musty congested smell of the small entrance hallway was not welcoming. My mother was creative and arranged the small bedroom to make it comfortable for the four of us. I began to realize that life as a Haitian immigrant would not be a fairytale while living in the United States.

Our first housing experience in the States was comprised of a single-family home which was sectioned into several rooms and rented to several tenants. There was only one bathroom to share with all these strangers who were mostly men. Needless to say, I was unimpressed. My mother reassured us that this arrangement was temporary, and she did keep her promise. We managed to move into a more desirable living arrangement three months later. Mom worked day and night to take care of us, and I never understood how she was able to afford everything with barely earning minimum wage.

Once we settled in Spring Valley, New York, I thought it was decided by my mother that my sister and I would attend the school associated within our district. I didn't understand the concept nor the regulations connected to attending only the school assigned to my community. My first day at Ramapo Senior High School was uneventful as I couldn't understand the foreign dialect that everyone insisted on speaking. I surely remembered taking required English courses in elementary school in Haiti, but the sound of the words was much faster and pronounced differently than I recalled. As I walked through the halls of my new high school headed toward my locker, I saw a girl that I recognized from my former elementary school in Port-au-Prince. We were inseparable when we attended school back in Haiti. I was so excited to see her, and I had the biggest smile on my face. I called out to Mikaelle; I couldn't believe that she was there. She looked at me, surely recognized me, but she walked away without saying a word. I didn't understand that speaking Creole was forbidden especially amongst the Haitians who wanted to dissociate themselves from their cultural ties, and most importantly, the ones who had chosen to lie about their exact origin.

My weird sense of fashion or lack thereof didn't help my social life. I loved my multi-colored clothing, although the combination of colors could have been more fitting for a Halloween party or a New Orleans carnival; my oversized blouse and baggy pants didn't do my 90-pound frame justice. This was my new reality, and I never liked being excluded or dismissed. I was determined to somehow find a way to fit in.

My relationship with the Haitian community was temporarily brought to a halt during my junior year of high school. I completely blocked my culture and its past, proceeding to fully embrace the American culture. Although most of my friends were Haitians, I consciously sought out to build relationships with cultural backgrounds other than my own. I was not content with my own identity, and I felt that rejecting my culture would be the first step toward creating a new character. It was quite easy to emulate others and wanting to fit into a crowd as opposed to standing on my own. I didn't want to be seen alone, so I joined my high school volleyball team and stumbled upon Guerline, a friend whom I had known from Haiti. We were both on the same wavelength, desperately seeking to belong to the cool kids' club.

I had a crush on Andy, our high school class president. He was smart, had the bluest eyes, and the whitest smile. Andy was one of the many white guys in my advanced French class. My crush for Andy never materialized into anything, but we became good friends. The memory of me discarding my French and Haitian cassette tapes is still vivid in my mind. I returned home one day from school, piled up the cassette tapes, along with some letters from friends and relatives and placed them in a large black garbage bag, never to be seen again. I stopped speaking French and rarely Creole, and eventually stopped writing letters to friends and family back home. I slowly removed myself from the world from which I was most familiar. I felt myself becoming more and more detached from my culture, as it became more comfortable for my mind to drift slowly into a new persona; a new identity had taken shape, one that I didn't quite recognize.

I reconnected with Bau during my junior year in high school. Bau and I remained in contact even after he left Haiti, despite my mother's efforts to prevent me from staying in touch with him. We often communicated via letters, which I kept hidden in my school bag, and we often spoke over the phone from time to time at Manou's house. His second letter was different than the first one he'd sent the month prior. Apparently, he'd begun to notice that I was becoming a woman and his interest began to develop into something far less platonic.

As the letters became more frequent, more poetic, and much more romantic, I found myself falling in love with the idea of him and what he represented at the time. He was much older than me, and he was giving me the attention that I desired. I was delighted to know that he lived in New York City, about 35 miles from Spring Valley.

One Saturday morning, I boarded the Red and Tan Lines toward 42nd Street, Port-Authority, NYC. I arrived at the station at 10:15 in the morning, making my way down the long moving stairs. I was behaving like a tourist, looking at everything with fresh eyes and amazement. As I walked through the station, I saw an older black man playing the guitar and singing *My Funny Valentine.* I stopped to listen to his soothing voice and wondered, why this talented man was not on stage performing for the world to see. I proudly dropped a dollar into the hat in front of him and continued walking toward some shops within the station. I noticed Au Bon Pain, and stopped there to get a hot chocolate and asked the cashier for directions to get to the Upper West Side. She gave me the option to either take a yellow cab or take the train. I settled on the train since it was much cheaper and within my budget. McDonald's was my first job here in the U.S., but my earnings were not much. I earned five dollars per hour and was only allowed to work 15 to 20 hours per week due to school and my many extracurricular activities.

I hopped on the Number 1 train heading to 96th Street, still packed with Saturday morning commuters. There was a man that looked to be in his mid-thirties preaching loudly, seemingly mad at the world, so I moved to another seat hoping to better position myself to see the signal for each stop. I grew anxious as someone unwittingly blocked my view, preventing me from deciphering the words of the conductor through the noisy speakers. As the "preacher" moved to another car, two young teenagers began break dancing as if they were the next crazy act to take the stage. Would I ever adapt to this new urban culture of bipolar preachers and break-dancing beggars? Perhaps I would be, judging by the passengers appearing to be unphased by all the obscure activities on the train. I felt lucky to have found a seat as my three-and-a-half inch heels began to unleash a blistering pain on my feet. I was hoping that Bau's house wasn't too far from the station as I did not bring flats along with me.

As I exited the train station, I was met by a group of people walking at a fast pace toward the train station. Everyone seemed anxious, which left me feeling quite unsettled. For some strange reason, it felt like I belonged there. I felt connected to the city, and I loved every minute of my trip thus far. I felt relief and excitement as I awaited Bau's arrival outside the 96th Station by a small coffee shop. I saw him appear before me and

for the first time, he seemed to be shorter than I rem
jeans, a turtleneck sweater, and a white bubble jacke
see him, but he definitely was entirely different from tl
I remembered.

We walked to his apartment not too far from the tı shared an apartment with his mother, but she wasn't there when we arrived. That day, Bau let his wall down and spoke to me candidly. He was attending a community college with the hope of going to medical school one day. He was now an immigrant, just like me, in the United States, trying to start over.

He appeared to have lost his commanding spark; he was no longer leading the crowd, but instead having acquiesced to the emasculating inevitability of life as a Haitian immigrant in New York City.

He appeared somewhat complacent and reluctantly content with his new life. He had become a mere shadow of himself, having to relearn and readapt, merely to remain barely visible. I felt that he was afraid to compete on the bigger stage of the world; he kept himself recused and somewhat stagnant. He was moving slowly, lagging behind and missing out on many opportunities that the Big Apple had to offer. The ambition that I once admired had vanished; his charm was no longer apparent, and my desire for him had dissipated.

I began to realize that most immigrants who lived in the United States struggled and it was harder for some to find a clear path because of a lack of guidance or resources. I was feeling sorrow for my Haitian community and pain for many who had lost their ambition and drive to succeed. Could this country be so cruel as to wash away our dreams of becoming something more? Will we no longer be in charge of charting our own path, but rather succumbing to the designated station that has been assigned to our community? Luckily for me, the answer was NO, as lucky.... I had a mother who sacrificed everything to open my doors and opportunities for my siblings and me. She did the dirty work like cleaning other people's lavish homes or provided care to the elderly so that I wouldn't have to. Nana was the love of my life, but my mother was so much more than a worthy replacement, and I was honored and thankful to have her in my corner.

Throughout my education, I began to form social circles of other immigrants who were medical doctors, engineers, and high-powered politicians who also migrated to the United States – all sharing their stories of how they struggled on a minimum wage income, just to make ends meet. I have always heard that America was the land of opportunities, but was this true? It was becoming clear that some of us were indeed taking advantage of the opportunities that were available to all who seek them, and I certainly intended on being one of them. Of course, there were circumstances I could never understand, like why an immigrant who was a doctor in their former country, would settle for becoming a caregiver here in the States. Perhaps that was just enough, and probably their happiness was not tied to their profession. I came to realize that living the American Dream meant having choices, and the freedom to make them. There is no perfect life or a perfect story. We immigrants simply adapt to an ever-changing narrative, and for most of us, these challenges made us resilient with success stories to be proud of.

Bau became more reachable and attainable as I was slowly becoming detached; my exposure to a new world had replaced my naïve admiration of him. Bau had become another boy navigating his way through the vast blue sea that was America. I saw him a couple more times after the New York City visit; once he came to visit me in Spring Valley, then finally, only sporadically in my thoughts.

CHAPTER FOUR

Thoughts of Fatherless Childhood

I didn't usually associate my past with my present behavior, but I was good at burying my pain and even better at keeping secrets. I always felt that focusing on my history would hinder my ability to move forward. I was still at war with myself, relishing at every negative thought which seemed to form an alliance against me. The haunting continued until the day that I finally met my father. It was while I still lived in Haiti, before coming to the States. It was a typical afternoon when one of my paternal cousins showed up on my doorstep with a letter. As she proudly handed the mysterious letter to my mom, she looked at me and said, "This is from your father." My eyes widened, and my heart was full of joy and excitement, but I refrained myself from expressing my contentment as I did not want to upset my mother. I was anxious to uncover the content of the letter as my mother was still casually chatting with my cousin and offered her some tea. She sarcastically muttered, "So Denis finally remembers he has a child."

My cousin protested and defended her uncle. "He is not the only one at fault. How long has it been anyway?"

"Long enough to have heard from him by now," my mother replied, her eyes sternly fixed on my cousin.

"Denis' daughter is practically grown. Look at your cousin."

I wasn't practically grown. I was 14, but I understood that in my mother's mind, I was close enough to 18 that a few years didn't make a difference. This was my father they were discussing, and I felt like I didn't have a say in the conversation. I listened to every word with curiosity and impatiently waited for my mother to open the letter. "Uncle Denis wanted to be sure you got his letter right away, and I've done that." My cousin looked at me when she said it. I wasn't sure if her words were directed at me or if it was sarcasm intended for my mother.

I was happy when my cousin finally made her exit. I was nervous but anxious, and I could tell that my mom shared the same feelings as she gazed at the letter for a long few seconds before she opened it. She read it silently, and the suspense was killing me. She finally handed the letter to me, and I rushed to read it. I was somewhat surprised by this sentence, "You've kept my daughter away from me for so long. Now it's time that I get to know her." Was my mother a contributing factor to keeping my father away from me? My father expressed how he loved me, he wanted to see me, and he was planning on visiting me soon and replacing my last name with his. I was somewhat mad at my mother but ecstatic that I was finally going to meet my father. I was lost in my thoughts when my mother said with relief in her voice, "So you are finally going to meet your father!" I was confused by my mother's reaction. If she kept me away from him for so many years, why was it so easy for her to allow me to see him now?

I was 14 when he visited Port-au-Prince from New York and requested to see me. My cousin once again came to my house and announced the arrival of my father from the States. This time, she addressed me directly, "Your father wants to visit you tomorrow." As I searched my mother's eyes for approval, I heard her say to my cousin, "What time tomorrow?" I couldn't explain my feelings of joy and sadness at the same time. I went to my closet and pulled out the pretty floral dress that my mother made for me. I wanted to be beautiful, I wanted my father to love me, and I wanted him to acknowledge me as his daughter. I anxiously waited at the door for the sound of his footsteps. When he showed up, I was relieved and nervous. I immediately noticed where I inherited my high cheekbones. He was slim like me, average height, and I welcomed his warm embrace. He hugged my mother briefly and chatted with her in a familiar tone. Interestingly, she was not angry. She was genuinely happy that my dad visited me. I was puzzled.

My dad was very affectionate. He looked at me, hugged me, held my hands, and told me that he loved me. "This dress is beautiful on you. Look how pretty you are."

I blushed and felt a nervous excitement before I mustered the courage to ask him, "Why did it take you so long to visit me?"

He said, "Sometimes life gets in the way." What exactly did he mean? His answers to most of my questions were rather vague. "Did you think about me?" I was curious and wanted to know if the man who helped conceive me ever thought about me.

"All fathers think about their daughters," he said, his expression indicating that maybe he did think about me. I had so many more questions to ask him.

"What about pictures? Did mom send you any pictures of me?" I wondered if he had a chance to see me grow up through pictures.

"You're exactly as I pictured. Tall. Elegant. Pretty." My father was charming, for sure. I expressed to him that I was happy that he was back in my life.

"I can't wait to spend some more time with you again."

He expressed the same sentiments. "The distance between us will make things difficult my daughter, but I want to see you and hear all about your friends, school and the things you like to do." It sounded good. Even though his eyes seemed to glisten and dance as he looked at me, I still did not feel a sense of reassurance; hence, my joy quickly turned into confusion. I thought the void would have dissipated, and all my questions would be answered when I finally met him, but there were too many unanswered questions and he wasn't able to provide the answers that I needed. One visit couldn't make up for 14 years of missed conversations, or a strong arm to lift me off the ground when I fell off my bike, but nevertheless, I was happy that he made his appearance, and was willing to bestow upon me his last name.

He told my mother he wanted to amend my birth certificate to reflect his last name; I could now identify as someone who is a product of two people. The other part of my existence was no longer an enigma. I was so excited and proud to have my father's last name; he had returned and rescued me from a life of obscurity...well, so I thought. Before my father left for the States, my mother provided him with all the required legal paperwork to amend my birth certificate to reflect his last name. After my dad visited Haiti, I did not hear from him for many months. One day, I decided to call him. I asked him about the birth certificate, and he simply told me that he did not have the time. "Life is not as easy as you think, darling. I am constantly working." He told me this quickly before he said goodbye and hung up the phone. I realized that day I was never going to have my father's last name, and reluctantly understood why mother may have kept him away for many years. Perhaps she was trying to protect me from being disappointed. Sadly, my dad seemed almost compelled to prove his loyal indignation to the reputation of some of the men of my country, with a false promise, and nearly constant disappointments. Another day, another broken promise, and more lies. Perhaps he was too busy fighting to overcome his designated stance as a poor immigrant in the United States. Either way, he had proven that I was not a priority, nor did he give any thought to how this would affect a 14-year-old child. He never bothered to follow through with his promises, so I gave up on waiting for him to keep them.

When I moved to the States, I made a conscious effort to visit my father. I honestly attributed his lack of responsiveness to the thousands of miles that kept us apart. My father was always loving and affectionate the few times I visited, but that was the extent of our relationship. He would often say, "You are beautiful. You are my favorite daughter." Once I left his house, I wouldn't hear from him for months unless I called him. He never reached out to me via telephone, and we never had an opportunity to spend quality time together. His lack of interest in getting to know me was apparent. Since I was always the one who went out of my way to see him, I stopped visiting him. The thought of spending time with my dad no longer made me happy. My relationship with him was not organic, and for the first time, I thought that perhaps my father did not desire to have a relationship with me; at least that's what I needed to believe so that I could let go of the idea of having a father. I had decided that having a father would only cause more confusion in my life, so when he did not reach out to me, I decided that I would walk away and not look back. It actually ended up being one of the most impactful moments in my life. My dad has actually made it easier for me to walk away from people that I deem toxic in my life.

The last time I saw my dad was at Kings County Hospital in Brooklyn, hooked up to a life support machine. My aunt called my sister Lu and me, whom I had met years earlier after I migrated to New York. Together, we were tasked with the decision to unhook my father from life support. How could I be expected to make such a monumental decision given our past? There I was in my mid-twenties, looking at this stranger sleeping peacefully in a cold hospital bed. As I stared off and drifted into my thoughts, I knew he was already dead. I couldn't feel pain or sadness; he was a stranger. I couldn't bring myself to touch his hands, to perhaps bring him some last-minute comfort. I stood there looking at this unfamiliar person that I wished I knew. All I felt was a sense of pity. I never cried for my father's passing. I couldn't cry.

One of the best gifts I inherited from my father was meeting my older sister, Lu. When I first moved to the States, I was told by my father that my sister, Lu, lived on Long Island, and he gave me her telephone number. I immediately reached out to her, and thankfully, she was very receptive and invited me to visit her. Our connection was instantaneous as it felt like we knew each other for a very long time. My big sister's smile was welcoming, and her signature high cheekbones resembled my father's as well. I also noticed that we both had our father's beautiful brown eyes. I took the opportunity to glimpse into my father's life, and soon discovered, that my sister too, was a fatherless child. "Bernie, I tried to get to know him, but he never put forth an effort to get to know me," she told me. "Can you believe that he didn't even want to walk me down the aisle? I can't forgive him for that," my sister painfully remembered. Although she had his last name, he was never present in her life, and unlike me, she somewhat resented him. I was personally indifferent. We quickly became friends, and it was a relief to have someone who could understand my thought processes relating to the father I never had. Although I have made myself believe that not having a father did not affect me emotionally, subconsciously I knew that I was deceiving myself.

I wanted to make every attempt to address any residual baggage related to my dad, and any issues that were preventing me from moving forward with my life, so I decided to see a therapist shortly after my dad's passing. I was still seeking answers, and I felt an internal emptiness, and frankly, I did not know how to deal with it. I thought a therapist would help me sort out my life, and somehow provide the answers I was seeking. I felt that there was something wrong with me, and perhaps a therapist could fix me. Consequently, that venture was short lived when the therapist drummed up a cliché diagnosis of my misfortunes as an adult being tied back to my father in some way. In my opinion, that was too generous of a notion to have been the responsibility of someone who I had very little interaction with or emotion toward. I always thought this was a poor excuse for people who wanted to hide behind a glass house, looking at the world from the inside. When I stopped going to the therapist, I realized that I had already forgiven my father as I no longer felt any anger or resentment toward him. Why was I still feeling so empty inside?

Back in my freshman year of high school, I was finally happy to see my mother with a companion after being alone for so many years. His name was Pierre. I often felt that she questioned some of the choices she made as a parent, without having a father figure present, so perhaps my mom would finally achieve the two-parent household that we deserved. I'd become quite close to the new man in my mother's life; I finally felt like I had a "dad" whom I looked up to and admired. Any waning feeling of longing for my biological father had all but dissipated. Pierre had three children of his own, two were around my age, and one not much younger than me. During one of our conversations, he said, "You are very mature for your age, and beautiful, too." Little did I know at the time that these kinds of statements weren't compliments. I am not sure whether he moved in with my mother because he wasn't working or simply because he wanted to be there. My sister, Patsy, never liked him as she felt that he was simply a "space taker." She hardly spoke to him. He always talked about his injury from work, and always thought that he would have a lot of money when his civil lawsuit would settle. He became a father figure to me, and I often confided in him, innocently seeking a paternal perspective. I talked to him about my love interests, how I would prefer to be married before I lose my virginity, and how I was excited to go to college. I was soon faced with the reality that Pierre had very little interest in being a father figure to me.

I usually tagged along with Pierre on his short drives, whether to the supermarket, or the park. Sometimes his daughter came along. There was one particular Saturday that Pierre asked me to accompany him to the park. He wanted to get some fresh air. I happily complied. I sat on a bench with a book in my hand, enjoying a perfect spring day. Pierre walked around the park for a few minutes and came back to sit next to me. He smiled and said, "Wow, you are going to college soon. That's something." I shook my head in agreement while still very much lost in my book. He proceeded, "I want to protect you from these low lives out there. I want to give you a gift." I became excited and turned my attention to him. He continued to express his feelings toward me, his sexual desires, and his words were explicit. My world was crushed when my mother's boyfriend told me that he wanted to be the one to take my virginity. He expressly set out to achieve his sadistic goal as I was preparing to head off to college. Just like most child molesters, Pierre attempted to wrap his fiendish desires into a manipulative bow, as if he were presenting a going away gift to me. That was the moment that I realized I was not "his little girl" as I naïvely desired. His eyes were determined, confident, and steady. You could tell that he was betting everything on the odds that I would fall for his scheme. As I broke his gaze, I slowly walked away in shock and disbelief. My shock quickly turned to tears, as I sobbed until my voice was no longer detectable. I often felt embarrassed about the fact that I was still a virgin. Could the traumatic interaction between Pierre and me be attributed to my feeling contrite about being a virgin?

My optimistic view of the world was somewhat distorted with suppressed thoughts that would somehow find their way back into my consciousness. These episodes hindered my relationship with my mother as she did not believe me initially when I confided in her. When I arrived home, I was still upset. I immediately rushed to tell my mother about the conversation that took place at the park. She paused and said in an angry and nervous tone, "I know that you guys don't like Pierre, but there is no reason to create such a big lie about him." I became angry and stormed out of the house. I went to my friend Kianna's house and confided in her. She believed me, and I always appreciated how she reassured me that everything was going to be ok. The more I tried to bury my thoughts, the more pain I felt. Most of the time, I couldn't remember why I was crying. I simply couldn't pinpoint the specific issue; this could not be normal, but was I normal? I hid my pain so much that I started to forget.

Not facing my fears, my truth and my disappointments contributed to the decline of my self-esteem. My decision-making became dubious at best, especially relating to relationships with men. I always considered myself very level-headed and cognizant, but I really had begun to question myself. I started feeling insecure, I doubted myself, and frankly, I did not know how to act around my male friends. I secretly questioned their intentions, and always wondered if there were some ulterior motives when they befriended me. Hiding my thoughts caused me so much grief, painful decisions, regrets, and created a sense of fear in my life.

I needed to recognize the issue at hand, face it and correct it. I needed to forgive myself and move forward, but that task wasn't as simple as it sounded. Somehow, I needed to accept that my self-esteem was brutally beaten, and I had no choice but to envision a clear path forward. My mind had been cloudy, unfocused, and lacked clarity. Funny enough, I felt that my heart and my soul had been working in direct conflict for years. They have failed to coincide most of the time, causing me great frustration and insecurity. I've always known that my mind was stronger than my heart. It was easier for me to control my thoughts without the unyielding investment of trailing my heart into it. In my opinion, the heart was weak and vulnerable… it wants to love and be loved, but that was not something that I could guarantee. In most situations, my mind had a sense of reasoning, whereas my heart made illogical decisions. When my mind and my heart were not in conflict, I wondered if I often made the wrong decision. Low self-esteem had often robbed me of my self-worth on more than a few occasions. How could I have possibly loved a man when I was so broken? Sometimes I often reflected on my childhood and wondered if I would have been a different person if I had my father's love. It was taking me a long time to put these pieces together, but I needed to put them together, and fast!

CHAPTER FIVE

Relationships Misunderstood

The following August after graduating high school, I arrived at Pace University Campus. I was happy and excited for what was to come. I applied to one single school based on the recommendation of one of my very close friends, Kianna. I did not understand how the whole college process worked in high school, and my guidance counselor's minimal help wasn't beneficial. I selected Pace University because Kianna was already there. I never considered how I would pay for the school or the possibility of not getting accepted. Kianna was the very first friend I met when I moved to the States. In fact, she was handpicked for me by my mother. My mother and her mom were long-time friends, so Kianna came with the package. I learned most of my initial English phrases from her. She had a big heart, was a strict Christian, and believed in the concept of sex after marriage. She even convinced me to visit her Pentecostal church with her a few times, while I was a devoted Catholic.

She was raised with both parents, had two siblings, and often had dinner together as a family. I spent a lot of time at her house, but she was extremely private about everything. I never stepped foot into her bedroom as it was off limits. I remember she had very few romantic relationships, and I never met her boyfriend. I was always the one divulging a few of my little dark secrets. It was at Kianna's house that I watched *Pretty Woman* for the first time and fell in love with the idea of the quintessential prince charming. Besides my Nana's fairytales, *Pretty Woman* and *The Sound of Music* became my second favorites. I noticed that Kianna's mother was the same way, a very secretive woman as well. I understood that she emulated her mother and was almost exactly like her. She was my closest friend, and I couldn't wait to join her at Pace University until I realized she attended the Pleasantville Campus and lived at home, while I was embarking on my journey alone at the New York City Campus with the help of a Pell Grant and thousands of dollars in student loans.

I didn't quite understand what to do with my new found freedom. I was 18, on my own with no parental supervision. Finally, I was an adult, and I could do whatever I wanted without the watchful eyes of my mother. I found myself sometimes crying at school for no particular reason, but I knew I was still battling with my demons internally. After I left home, I did not go back for months, nor did I speak to my mother. I stayed away for almost a year, even though my mother tried to reach out to me many times. I eventually visited my mother when I heard that she was no longer with Pierre.

I was introduced to a pair of twins by a mutual friend. I never met them in person before enrolling at Pace University, but I recognized them while walking to take my seat on the second row to watch the Pace University men's basketball team play against some other team whose name I don't recall. I saw these two pretty girls with chocolate brown skin and the most beautiful smiles. I called them by name, not knowing which one was Ella or Jane, and we immediately started talking like we had known each other for years! They were both accounting majors and were very conservative. They always chose their words carefully. Their hearts were pure, and they were the kind of friends who were sincere, trustworthy, and smart. They were not the type of girls who dated a lot in college. They believed in the definition of "Mr. Right." We would often eat together when we didn't have conflicting schedules.

I remembered one time I must have consumed some spoiled food from the cafeteria. I stopped by the twin's dorm room for a chat. For some unknown reason, a loud, conspicuous fart slipped out! All I could do was laugh hysterically. Ella and Jane had somewhat of a nervous smile, and they both walked toward me, and one grabbed me by my arms and the other by my legs, dragging me out of their room. We laughed so hard, and I remembered this moment as one of the most memorable times we spent together. Ella and Jane were the type of friends who could listen to my issues and calmly advise me how to approach the situation logically. They were level-headed. I was happy to have met them. I started to understand that their friendships would have a profound impact on my life. They became part of my support system and brought a lot more laughter in my life.

I was once again introduced to love as a young adult during rush hour on the steps of a New York City Subway. My first "real" kiss was so subtle and beautiful. As I was walking back to my dorm room, he tapped me on my shoulder, right before the last step of the stairway, and kissed me passionately. I could never forget that face, and he thought I was beautiful. His name was Rafy. I met him while I was walking to the metro station on my way to Brooklyn. He was my Denzel for a short time, perhaps because he was the one who introduced me to *Mo' Better Blues*, which I must have watched a thousand times.

I remember taking a walk with him to the South Street Seaport on a breezy summer night; he always insisted that I walk on the right side of him. I didn't know what this meant at the time, but I thought he was sweet and kind. Had I known how to love then, could he have been my soulmate? My lack of confidence always had a way of blocking my sunshine. In fact, everywhere I stood, there was a cloud. I didn't even know I was beautiful. Although I always had an optimistic view of the world, the internal antagonist won many battles against my confused mind. I also thought my virginity was an obstacle, and quite frankly, my primary goal in my freshman year of college was to free myself of that 'burden.' It was ironic how unpopular I felt because I was a virgin in college.

I was adamant about losing my virginity. Even the wisdom of my 18-year-old best friend, Anne, couldn't convince me not to proceed with my agenda. She knew then that intimacy was sacred and interconnecting energy, and body fluids were meant to be shared with someone special. I met Anne through a summer program I attended at Pace University in Briarcliff, New York. She was pretty with light caramel skin and the prettiest long flowing hair. She was fit as she loved to dance. She must have been 110 pounds. She knew she was beautiful. Our friendship started that summer.

I had a way of letting everyone know how to pronounce my last name. I would stand up in the middle of a lecture hall with hundreds of people, and say "JEUDY" in the most distinctive French Haitian accent every single time a professor or a student mispronounced my name. Anne found me quite annoying, mainly when I performed my pronunciation act toward the end of the lecture when everyone was rushing to get food. By the fourth day of the program, we had lunch together, we talked, and we realized we were not so different after all.

Anne was born in Guyana and raised in Canada by her single mother. She also had her Indian grandmother who loved her. Anne was kind, had a good heart, and her free spirit was one of her best qualities. She reminded me of me when I danced in the rain in Gommier. I wondered how I let this free-spirited little girl that I once knew escape my soul. We were both teenagers trying to figure out college life. We became inseparable, and we often had lunch together. After the two-week program ended, we happily said goodbye as we knew we would see each other again during the fall semester at Pace University in the incredible New York City campus. Another chapter of my life began.

As luck would have it, Anne and I had English 112 together. The class was taught by the infamous Professor Israel. She had a reputation for being a harsh grader. Most students had confirmed that her C grades were generous at best and that she expected the highest level of work from her students. Being trilingual, my thought process was always in French and Creole. I challenged myself, and I certainly did not like the letter C, especially as a grade for English. The first essay was to write about something that evoked emotions, so I wrote about my father and received a B+. I was explaining my disappointment to Anne and telling her that Professor Israel was unfair, that I should have gotten an A-. Anne looked at me and said, "You are nuts." We both started laughing and headed to the cafeteria for a quick bite.

I cherished the memories of loud noises, the combination of people talking and the train conductor screaming over an inaudible microphone. The underground of the New York City Subway was always hot even in the wintertime. I felt Rafy's touch over my hand alerting me that we had arrived at our destination. I had decided to move out of my dorm room at Pace University to explore living on my own in Brooklyn. I've always had the desire to be an adult, especially during high school. I couldn't quite pinpoint why other than perhaps I wanted to be in charge of my own destiny. My dorm room was fully paid for by financial aid, whereas I had to pay for my place in Brooklyn out of pocket from my part-time job. My thinking wasn't logical.

Rafy walked me home from the Number 2 train, and I invited him to come inside my $400 rented small bedroom located on Utica Avenue. He was somewhat taken back that I lived in that area. I didn't quite understand the difference between good and bad neighborhoods in New York City. The narrow hallway that led to my bedroom always had a distinct smell of old, overcooked, greasy food. We passed several closed doors, a broom closet, and a freshly used mop that gently rested along the yellow stained wall. My landlord must have been working, and I was relieved she was not there. When we finally entered my room, we were immediately greeted by a mouse resting comfortably on my wooded twin-size bed. The bed was a gift from my friend, Jeanne. I was horrified! I was embarrassed, but at the same time, I was laughing hysterically. I vividly recalled the mouse running to hide in my closet. Rafy wanted me to open my closet, but I refused. The thought of everything falling out of my sufficiently cluttered closet would have been much more embarrassing than the mouse on my bed. Although I kept my 300-square foot room clean, my environment was somewhat chaotic. All the clutter was uncomfortably hidden in my closet, and now the mouse had joined the disorder. *"I'm definitely moving back to the dorm,"* I concluded.

Despite the embarrassment of the moment, Rafy remained with me. I remember sitting still next to him on my twin bed. I looked at the bare white walls and tons of school books in the corner of my small undecorated bedroom. I wanted to gaze at his beautiful caramel complexion, his light brown eyes, and his killer smile, but my shyness and embarrassment forced me to keep my eyes fixated on the wall. I wasn't particularly looking at anything. Many thoughts of insecurity were going through my mind. What did he think of me? Did he still like me? Was I going to see him again? Would he ever call me back? I was more concerned about his feelings toward me than my confidence in myself. My emotions were not relevant at that moment. How could I even consider how I felt when I was so insecure? It was all about how Rafy felt.

He stayed, hugged me, and he must have loved my long flowing hair as he complimented me a few times. Now that I look back, Rafy was not even erected. I assumed a running mouse would temporarily remove all sexual desires from a man's mind. Rafy was very connected to his Afro cultural roots, which I did not understand at the time. All I knew was my desire to adapt to European culture. This adopted French culture was always an imposition on every aspect of my life. I remember in grammar school in Haiti, I was forbidden to speak Creole. I would be severely punished had I broken the rules.

Lost in my thoughts, I couldn't remember whether Rafy's hands felt sensuous, or whether I felt his gentle touch and kisses. My mind was racing at a thousand miles per hour, and instead of enjoying the moment, I was worried about the end of my relationship with him. Suddenly I screamed, feeling his penis penetrating me. I could imagine how terrifying it must have been for Rafy, as my agonizing scream could have awakened my neighbors. He stopped immediately because he was visibly frightened, as he did not know I was a virgin.

I apologized for my pain as Rafy was tensed and didn't say a word. He simply held me. I tried to remedy the situation by attempting to satisfy him with my awkward fellatio; he would not let me as he gently pulled my head away. He hugged me silently. I confused his reaction with rejection. This was a chance for me to lose my virginity, and he rejected me, I thought. I began to believe that my virginity was a curse. I was relentless to get rid of it, and two weeks later, I told him I did not want to see him anymore. I was confused and a messed-up teenager. I initiated the breakup, yet I cried for many months over him, and like many teenagers in love, I allowed him to occupy a permanent spot in my brain for a long time.

My best friend, Anne, always scolded me and reminded me that intimacy should be shared with someone special. It is an exchange of positive and negative energy. I was somewhat stubborn, and once my mind was made up, it was challenging to deviate from my plans. The words of my best friend did not quite make sense at the time, and I did not realize that some things in life needed to happen organically and not be forced. Come to think of it, I've always been a rigid planner, which resulted in many failures, heartbreaks, and unnecessary tears that could have been easily avoided. Sex and losing one's virginity should not have been in my plans. I should have allowed life to happen and enjoy all the exciting moments of college life without the pressure of having sex or losing my virginity.

Over the years, I have pleased many people, never comfortable with saying no. I didn't want to disappoint anyone; therefore, my discomfort was validation that I was making someone else happy. I was always eager to please, thinking I was being that "sweet girl" often forgetting to consider myself. I was desperately seeking approval and acceptance. I lacked confidence, and the word "NO" was unknown to me. My kindness was often mistaken for weakness. I was taken for granted and manipulated. The thought of saying "NO" to anyone was unimaginable, and the more I said yes, the weaker I became. The more I said yes, the more money I spent. The more I said yes, the more broke I became. The more I said yes, the more I didn't like myself. I came to the realization that "yes" was not my strength. YES was my weakness.

CHAPTER SIX

Intimacy Confused with Love

It was a chilly winter evening as I walked toward Canal Street. There was something about the crowded streets of New York City that always made me feel alive. Ironically, I did not even like crowds, but Manhattan was unique. There was an unusual love affair between The Big Apple and me. We always found a way to reconcile our differences, and I must confess, I have been unfair to her. I have even blamed New York for some of my shortcomings. Still, the beautiful Manhattan always made me feel so alive as I navigated my way through my young life. Chinatown was a happy place, welcoming the curious tourists around the clock.

The foodies and tourists were still enjoying every bite of the over-cooked duck meat hanging behind the glass windows of several small Chinese restaurants along Canal Street. Somehow living in New York City had always made me happy. The skyscrapers had a weird way of dancing to the reflection of the beautiful illuminating lights of the city even on a cold, windy night. I often smiled as I perfected the illusion of happiness. I buried all negative thoughts deep down in my brain. I eventually believed I was a gleeful person.

My hands were frozen. I should have taken the winter gloves that I bought a week earlier from a thrift shop in Chelsea. I didn't want to go back to my dorm room, so I continued toward the A train. Thankfully the subway arrived on time. I was headed to my friend Anne's house. The conductor of the train yelled through the microphone, "14th Street Union Square Station." Another transfer I thought. I jumped on the 4 train to Nevins Street and transferred to the Number 2 to the final stop in Brooklyn. It was about 7:30 in the evening, and I was full of energy when I arrived at Anne's house that Saturday. I often traveled to Anne's house to eat a home-cooked meal whenever my meal card ran out, and for a while, I stopped going home. We often laughed when we sat together at a round table in the large cafeteria. A conversation during meals was one of the ways of releasing all the pressure that came with college life. We laughed, cried sometimes, and talked about boys whenever we had a chance to be together.

I devoured the curry stew that Anne's mother, Mrs. Cooks, made. I sat and listened to the jazz, appreciating every note of the music that Anne's stepfather was playing. The smoothness of the trumpet and bass and the strong vocals that narrated the love stories were exactly what I longed to be true for my life. Listening to jazz music at Anne's is where I discovered the legendary Miles Davis, Minnie Riperton, and Nat King Cole. I started to develop a promising friendship with jazz, and the soothing sound gave me a sense of peace that I hadn't felt before. Anne had a younger sister, Jivie, and a younger brother, Miles – named after Miles Davis. Taking in the music, I heard Anne's voice telling me to get ready as we decided to venture the streets of New York City on a beautiful cold Saturday night. The year was 1994. I quickly got dressed in clothes that I had packed as I intended to spend the weekend in Brooklyn. I also bought my books to study with Anne as we had three classes together.

I skipped the hairdresser that Saturday. My American Express Card was maxed out, and I had misplaced my faithful Visa. Credit cards were easily attainable in college. During my first day of orientation, I was approved for three credit cards. I just understood that I had money available to spend and didn't realize the complexity of newly acquired debts. That night, I decided to wear the wig I purchased earlier that week. I always wanted my hair to look like the short cut that Whitney Houston sported throughout her musical career, and since my hair was long, and I wasn't yet ready for the sound of unfriendly scissors, I decided to wear my wig. I wore my little black bodycon dress purchased from my favorite thrift shop in Chelsea. I also wore tights and a long pair of boots. Anne and I met three other friends nearby as they had a car. We were young, not entirely innocent, still very much confused about life, and we were ready to party.

As I walked toward the club with my friends, the cold wind was unforgiving. My wig decided to part ways with my hair! I quickly ran into the streets to recover what remained of my wig after a fast-moving car decided to flatten it. I heard my friends' hysterical laughs as I rejoined them with my destroyed wig in my hand. Thankfully my hair was nicely pulled back. I removed the wig cap as we approached the club. I placed the wig in my oversized black purse. I must say that the bouncer was strangely confused when he inspected my bag. He slowly took the synthetic hair out and held it up, and carefully examined it as if it were a foreign object, while a long line of strangers waited to get into this crowded NYC nightclub. My wig brought a lot of laughter that night. This was a night I will never forget. Anne and I often joked about that fateful night.

As long as you are alive, you are bound to have an unplanned encounter; well, let's just say that night changed my life forever. After we danced until the wee hours of the morning, we were famished. I wanted to sleep while my friends were adamant about going to a local diner at 4:00 am for the quintessential hangover breakfast food. Nothing beats greasy eggs, pancakes, thick corn syrup, and white toast after a long night of dancing and drinking. Interestingly, I never thought about how this kind of food would affect my body and my health years later. I remembered telling Anne that I wanted to stay in the back seat of the high-mileage black Mazda and peacefully catch up on my beauty sleep, but Anne was very convincing and insisted that I tag along. I reluctantly went to the diner, and my sleepiness was gone with the early cold morning breeze.

After I placed my order for cinnamon pancakes, eggs, two slices of tomatoes and cheese, I went to use the restroom. IHOP was full of club goers, mostly young and tired teenagers. I bumped into a close by table, and the person at the table dropped their fork. I immediately said, "I am sorry," and my heart almost skipped a beat when I noticed a handsome man walking toward my direction. I stopped between two tables closer to the bathroom. I looked back to curiously peek at the woman he was walking toward as he smiled. Was he smiling at me? My legs felt weak, and I mustered the courage to walk faster. He said, "Excuse me, Miss." He had a radiant smile that quickly captured my attention. He was about 6'2" and very easy on the eyes. I beamed with an inviting smile. He continued to approach me and said, "My friend Kevin wanted me to give you his number, but I figured I'd give you mine instead." This is how I met Michael. I smiled, and took the encrypted napkin, giving him an indication that I would call him, as I continued my way to the bathroom. There were those encounters that remained brief, and there were those that permanently changed my path.

I was slowly becoming a woman. I wasn't sure why I did not give Michael my number that night but gladly took the white piece of the napkin with his telephone number scribbled on it. I couldn't wait to call him the next day. I had a way of making things easy for people, especially for men. I always felt that I shouldn't complicate things, as though I was somehow 'cool.' Over the years, I've learned that people appreciate and value more the things they acquire through hard work, and men appreciate women who display confidence, high self-esteem, and self-worth. For whatever reason, my memory of my first love, the boy next door, totally escaped my mind, and I forgot how I was supposed to be treated. I forgot that the courtship was beautiful. It was that 'thing' that slowly gave a man access to a woman's mind and heart—something I completely skipped during my journey into adulthood.

I made everything easy for Michael. He did not have to work to earn my respect, my friendship, my intimacy, my touch, and my sense of caring. I made myself easily accessible to him. There were no date nights, no candlelight dinners, or walks in the park. Michael was physically there, in my bed, almost every day and for me, that was enough. Every time my body screamed with excitement, or my knees felt weak, or my heart beat a little faster, I thought I loved him. With Michael, I felt pleasure although I did not know what an orgasm was at the time, nor did I ever experience one while I was with him. I remembered his sensual touch, and at that moment, I felt like a woman. I was innocently confusing sexual intimacy with love.

CHAPTER SEVEN

Premature Motherhood

I went to visit Michael in his basement apartment in Brooklyn. On this particular evening, I wasn't in the mood to jump into his bed. I sat on a chair against the wall. I didn't feel particularly sexy that night. The daily morning sickness gave me an indication that something was terribly wrong. I felt sick to my stomach. My eyes were watery, and my throat was tightened. I wanted to talk, but I couldn't correctly get the words out. I pulled out the First Response pregnancy test and showed it to Michael. The two pink lines clearly said it all. I was pregnant! Michael's first reaction was for us to get married and to provide a traditional upbringing for the child. I did not welcome the news of the pregnancy with all smiles; my young mind was unable to think logically, and I thought my life was surely over. I was scared, but unafraid because I wasn't alone. I had Michael, and he was my unborn child's father. He hugged me that night then pulled himself away to ponder on the bombshell that I had just dropped. We both sat there in silence. He eventually asked me to leave, and with that, I left and headed back to my dorm room.

Michael was from Rochester, NY, and had moved to NYC for his first job. For a while, he lived with his roommate, Kevin, who trusted

Michael to get my telephone number for him. His roommate kicked him out when he came home one day to find Michael and me in his bed naked, evoking the name of the Almighty God because the sexual pleasure was too intense. Michael was from a somewhat dysfunctional family. His mother escaped from an abusive relationship with Michael's biological father. She later remarried to a loving man who raised Michael as his own son. It was difficult for his mother to let go of the trauma that she had experienced while she was with Michael's father. She made sure that she reminded Michael of his dad's abusive actions and past indiscretions quite frequently. Michael's biological father almost killed his mother. I often felt that he was a constant reminder of his father's disappointment in his mother's eyes.

Michael exhibited self-doubt and was fighting his own insecurities, lack of self-love, and self-confidence. In a way, he was also trying to find himself miles away from home, and I could imagine the unplanned pressure of fatherhood had become a burden that was too heavy for him to carry at the time. Perhaps Michael also thought New York City had all the answers he was seeking. I realized that Michael never truly loved himself, and he indeed wasn't as confident as he had appeared to be on that fateful night I met him at the IHOP restaurant.

The next day, Michael came to my dorm. "We need to talk." He spoke as he passed by me, not even looking at me in the eye. From his demeanor, I knew this couldn't be good. "Ok, do you want something to drink?" I offered. I was nervously bracing myself for what he was about to say. He must have had time to reflect on our conversation and realized the challenge that we were about to tackle in our early twenties. He appeared unusually distant and somewhat cold toward me. I didn't sleep well that night, as I had no idea how to handle the concept of a baby that was slowly growing inside my womb.

I experienced a deeper level of sadness that I couldn't quite explain. It seemed that my throat was steadily closing and my tears were never far away. I wished that my mother had talked to me openly about sex and pregnancy. Then again, how could she have when she probably didn't even know herself. Michael handed me a pamphlet without saying a word. He didn't even sit down. I quickly glanced at it with tears in my eyes. It was about the steps to take after an abortion. I was frankly surprised as we already discussed our plans the previous night. He broke his silence. "I'm too young to be someone's father. I barely make enough money to support myself, and I still have another year of college left. I can't do this." Michael asked me to have an abortion because he was young, broke, and scared.

My sadness intensified, and the frog in my throat prevented me from expressing my disappointment. The thought of aborting the baby never crossed my mind, because my view regarding abortion was different back then.

"I don't believe in abortions." I tried hard to fight back another burst of tears. "It's a sin." I somehow believed that God was going to punish me if I dared to commit such a "crime." Interestingly, I didn't feel the same way about having sex before marriage. I guess somehow, I was selective with my sins.

Michael said, "Then this is a choice you have to make alone. I can't be a father now."

I wiped the tears that were overpowering my face with my bare hands, and at that moment, I realized I was utterly alone. My biggest fear had finally become my reality. I was about to give birth to a fatherless child. I broke down, and I tried to hold on to Michael as he stormed out of my dorm room. He left, but the coldness of his visit remained in the room. I couldn't move; I sobbed until I fell asleep. I didn't go to any of my classes that day.

My college years were briefly interrupted as I prepared myself to embark into my journey of motherhood. Having a child was not an easy decision for me. I worried so much about people's opinions and what they might have thought of me. I could not explain the emptiness I felt. I was mostly at peace only when I fell asleep, and my mind was blank. I made sure I slept a lot. When I was awake, my mind was working at the speed of light. My Haitian mother was expecting a college degree. Instead, I had to find a way to tell her that I was pregnant during my second year of college. I confided in my brother, Hody, first. We orchestrated a plan on how to tell my mother and decided on, "Mom, I am not feeling well. I think I am pregnant." Surprisingly she didn't scream or yell. Maybe she understood the shame and sadness I was already experiencing. At that moment, I felt a sense of regret for having judged her, and I wondered how she must have felt when the father of her first child walked away from her. I started to understand and somewhat relate to her hidden sadness. My mother's support was invaluable, and the fact that she was there for me throughout the whole pregnancy, made my new reality a bit more tolerable.

I remember it as clear as yesterday. It was a typical Friday afternoon. While I was sitting on the couch watching one of my favorite shows, I felt an incredible pain which would later be described as contractions. I never attended those special Lamaze classes, and YouTube was not yet created, so I learned very little about pregnancy; besides, all I wanted to do during the entire pregnancy, was sleep, work, and sleep. My brother, along with my mother, rushed me to the hospital. While I was in my wheelchair waiting to be seen by a doctor, I caught a glimpse of a loving couple right next to me. There was so much love between them. I wondered how life would be, raising a child without a father. Tears of sadness again reminded me that I was all alone, an unmarried young black female was now about to become part of the doomed U.S. statistic of unwed mothers. I wanted to scream as I felt a sharp pain in my abdomen. I wanted and needed Michael to be here. I did not know where he lived as I stopped talking to him the minute he walked out and told me he was not ready to be a father. I even changed my phone number.

Was I becoming like my mother? She would often talk about how proud she was to be independent and could care for her children on her own. I fought that idea. I hated it. The thought was piercing through my brain and making each contraction more unbearable. My child must have a father, I thought to myself. Between epidural shots, doctors, and nurses telling me to push, I suddenly heard a faraway cry of a baby. I noticed that she had a big head, and I wondered whether her head would shrink in a few days. I didn't hold her. I just fell asleep. I was so tired.

After my daughter was born, I knew I would do her a great disservice to deprive her of her father. I expressed to my family my desire to reach out to Michael, but my mother insisted that I leave Michael in the past and focus on the present. I felt at least I owed it to my daughter to try and give her what I never had. I found out, through his former landlord, that Michael had moved back to Rochester, but I didn't know his address nor his phone number. These were the times when the white pages were still useful. I found a telephone number for a close relative. She gave me his home address, and I took a picture of my daughter. I put my pride aside, and I took my favorite blue pen and wrote on the back of the photo, *"This is your daughter. This may be the only picture you'll ever receive of her."* My heart palpitated as I inhaled and took a deep breath. I found the courage to mail only the picture in a small square white envelope with my return address clearly encrypted. I expected nothing, but I felt that I did the right thing, and time would determine if I was right.

Two weeks later, I received a telephone call. It was from Michael. He called my cousin in Brooklyn to get my telephone number. My heart nearly stopped. He sounded excited and confirmed that he would visit the following Friday. I looked at my small little creation sleeping in her crib in my mother's two-bedroom apartment and felt a little relief that at least her last name on the birth certificate would change one day.

Michael kept his word and was at my doorstep that Friday at precisely 2:45 in the afternoon. I honestly didn't know how to react. I said hello and introduced him to my family and walked him to his daughter's crib. He just stood still, staring at her with amazement. Maybe he realized that he was a contributing factor to creating a life, a little person, a beautiful little girl. He smiled and remained silent.

When I first saw him looking over the crib, I moved a little closer and stood next to him, looking at our beautiful baby girl. I felt a sigh of relief, knowing at least she had a father. Deep down inside, I longed for a typical family and hoped that perhaps someday, Michael and I could get back together and create our own. I envisioned the plan in my head, even before I had a conversation with Michael.

Naturally, I assumed this was how things would transpire, and without hesitation, I consciously created a space in my life for him. I let the door open, and he was back in my life without a fight, and we started back just where we left off. We never defined our relationship, we never talked about the past, and we never spoke about the future. I allowed things to happen organically while I harbored every frustration, anger, and sadness internally. Michael decided to move back to Spring Valley to be closer, so we rented a condominium not too far from my family, and we started our new life together.

It was hard to adjust to this new life as I had no idea how to cohabitate with a man, and I certainly did not know how to be a mother to my child. There was a sense of shame that was still hanging over my head. I felt as if I had done something wrong. For whatever reason, there was a sense of guilt that took over me. Perhaps deep down inside, I resented him for walking away, but I never brought the subject up since he came back into my life. I was the poster child of forgiveness, and I pretended that nothing traumatic ever happened between us. I never spoke up. I just showed Michael once again how I wanted him to treat me. I once again showed him I was a girl who couldn't even try to earn his respect.

Michael and I had discussed the idea of getting married because we wanted to legitimize our daughter. There was not much thought or planning given to such an important decision. I did not consult anyone. I remember feeling a little excitement over the idea of marriage, not because I loved Michael, simply because I just wanted to be married. I needed people to view me differently, and I wanted them to stop judging me. Perhaps this whole idea of society judging me was purely self-inflicted. Could it have been possible that people had so little to do in their everyday lives that they needed to fill their day by focusing on my life?

Michael and I decided to drive to Rochester to visit his parents. Michael's parents were not initially happy with the news of being grandparents; however, it appeared that everybody became more accepting as the idea of a baby started to sink in. I felt uneasy spending the weekend at his parents' house. I wanted to read their minds and was also concerned about how they may have perceived me. I couldn't fall asleep in the guest bedroom that was adjacent to Michael's room. Michael and

I stayed in separate bedrooms. My mind wandered while staring at the white ceiling until my eyes became heavy, and I didn't fall asleep until around 5:00 in the morning.

While Michael and I were in Rochester visiting his parents, we decided to obtain a marriage certificate. I was going to get married, but I never remembered being engaged. I guess we had skipped that step. I looked at the marriage certificate and contemplated the line with my last name, and I felt a sense of contentment that I was about to replace it with a man's last name. For some odd reason, the thought of marrying him frightened me, but at least my daughter would be legitimate.

Michael and I soon found out that we were not compatible and cohabitation was a bad idea. Neither one of us had the slightest idea of how a relationship between us would've worked. We clearly didn't love each other, but somehow our sexual compatibility kept the relationship going longer than it should have. We were both on different paths and had separate lives. We acted as if we were still single. I didn't like the way things were between Michael and me; however, I became so detached that I didn't care. Some weekends, I would go to Anne's house just to escape my dull life. Since my mother lived very close by, it was easier to go out as I could quickly drop off my baby daughter, Chrystie.

I arrived at the Spring Valley bus station, parked my car, and was waiting for the 11A local bus to come, but it dawned on me that I had forgotten a package that I promised Anne. I didn't want to go back home, but I forced myself to drive back to the apartment. I noticed Michael was laying down in the living room carpeted floor, his head totally covered with a blanket. I didn't want to wake him up, so I proceeded to my bedroom to get the package. I was thirsty and decided to go to the kitchen to get a bottle of water. As I was walking through the living room, I glanced at the unpaid bills piled up on the wooden coffee table. I remembered that I needed to mail the check for the electricity bill, so I stopped to grab the bill when I noticed a long synthetic hair braid peeking out from under the comforter where Michael was silently sleeping. I knew Michael would have never braided his hair, especially with synthetic hair. My innate instincts pushed me to react.

I pulled the comforter off him, not knowing what to expect. I saw Michael and his guest both naked, laying there silently, perhaps hoping that I wouldn't notice them. I was shocked, and I did not know how to react. I stood there, looking at them with widened eyes. I knew our relationship was not great, and I felt that at some point we would part ways, but surprisingly I never expected to see him having intimate re-lations with another woman in the space that we shared together with our two-year-old daughter. "How could you do this to me?" I managed to say. I could have probably answered my own question. I knew that Michael never loved me; he didn't respect me, and he didn't care to protect me. Frankly, I did not love him either as I never really got to know him on a deeper level beyond sexual intimacy. I was upset, but I did not feel anger.

I pretended that I wasn't hurting, but deep inside, I considered this episode another failure. I blamed myself. I didn't know how to love a man, and I had no idea how to learn. The woman that was with Michael was embarrassed and kept on apologizing. He got off the floor and harbored the woman, thinking that I would probably lose my mind and react.

"This is not what you think it is." He muttered a line that I have heard a thousand times in the movies, except this was my life, and I was wide awake.

I looked at her with sympathy and said, "This is not your fault." I walked out of the apartment, knowing that I had no other choice at the time but to move back with my mother.

Breaking up with Michael wasn't hard, but when he filed for sole custody of my only child, that ignited a fire within me. My fighting instinct took over, and that day, I indeed became a mother. After my daughter was born, I had a difficult time with the thought of being a mother. I relied on my mother to raise my daughter and guide her. I was somewhat ashamed and even more confused than ever. It wasn't always easy for me to freely divulge that information to perfect strangers. I always wanted to have a traditional family with a husband, a home, and children. I soon understood that life doesn't usually happen the way that I imagined. The curveballs were inevitable, and sometimes getting up from a fall took longer than I would have liked.

The thought of losing my daughter pushed me to fight for her. My $25,000 salary wasn't enough to cover the expenses and also hire an attorney, but I knew I needed to find one. I stopped thinking about all the obstacles and started thinking about solutions. I managed to find an attorney who agreed to a payment arrangement. I hated going to court, and I felt overwhelmed and exhausted, but every time I stepped in that courtroom, I became stronger. The idea of Michael having sole custody of my daughter and moving away with her back to Rochester kept me awake most nights. Not only was I dealing with a custody battle, but I was also stressed out about keeping my grades up as I had returned to school to finish my undergraduate degree. I was too afraid of losing my job because I took so much time off. After many months of court dates, psychological evaluations, many home visits, and court-appointed interviews, I was finally awarded sole custody of my daughter, and Michael had visitation rights.

I allowed Michael to be very much involved in Chrystie's life. I wasn't rigid with the court order as I still wanted him to be active in her life. He was a good father, and he loved his little girl, and for that,

I was thankful. Indeed, there was a good reason why I crossed paths with Michael. He entered my life at the right place and at the right time. Michael contributed to the most important achievement of my life, my beloved Chrystie. I began to be thankful for every experience as I started to understand that there was no such thing as meeting a person by accident or by pure coincidence. The people that crossed paths with me were meant to touch my life in some way, whether positively or negatively.

At times I felt as though I was focused too much on how long the person remained in my life rather than how much value the person added to my life. I concluded that every encounter could be translated into a valuable life lesson—lessons that could shape my life. I often missed these lessons, but I indeed became wiser and stronger with every experience. I've learned to allow people to exit my life gracefully when the time came. One thing that always stayed with me was that I would never force someone to love me or to stay with me.

My realization that love is not forced but comes naturally had become my new rule to live by. I learned to let go of the people who have served their purpose in my life. I tried not to create valuable space in my life for someone who no longer deserved a spot. I made sure I focused more on my career and my financial stability. I desired a better experience for my daughter and me; so, I started to rely solely on myself as I continued to move through life with the hope that the next encounter would be a better match for me.

CHAPTER EIGHT

Allowing Love to Slip Away

I glanced at my small ½ carat diamond ring and was content as I knew that he had used his tax refund money to acquire it. It was meant to be a symbolic gesture to solidify what I already knew; he loved me. He wasn't working at the time. He proposed to me in a non-ceremonious way, after a pointless argument during our very first international vacation together in Cancun, Mexico. I was still blinded by the materialistic view of society and of what was considered acceptable. As happy as I was with my less than perfect diamond ring, I often wondered what my friends would have thought of my rather minuscule diamond cut. Since I was a traditional girl with unconventional ideas, I decided that I didn't want any bridesmaids. I looked beautiful when I tried on my light cream lace princess dress and my modern fashionable veil. My wedding was going to be unique, only to be witnessed by my closest friends and family and of course, my dearest friend and matron of honor, Anne.

I reserved an older mansion in White Plains, as I visualized how beautiful a large vase of white roses would have looked on the center of each table. I imagined my friends and family dancing on the shiny refurbished hardwood floors. I even played my eclectic first song choice,

'Butterflies' by Michael Jackson. The sweet smell of vanilla scented candles overpowered the room while I danced with my 'soon to be husband' for the first very first time. I planned every detail, from floral design, photography, food, napkins, tablecloths, and the selected guest list. I meticulously planned the perfect wedding, while I completely forgot about the man that I was preparing to marry. I was slowly allowing love to slip away, as I scanned the empty room one last time wondering what could have been.

I met Jay at a nightclub in New York City, precisely one year and two months after Michael and I parted ways. This was the first time I had a chance to spend some quality time with myself. I had since developed a stronger bond with my daughter. I always heard that people say it was technically impossible to find love and build a committed relationship with someone you met in a nightclub, but my story told otherwise. As with Jay, I learned to date. I allowed him to pursue me and spend quality time with me, and I didn't feel the need to rush the process. The courtship felt terrific, and he made me feel special. Our first date was simple yet unique. We grabbed brunch from a street vendor in New York City while we explored the beauty of my favorite city on a beautiful fall day. Afterward, we drove up to Nyack River in his red BMW convertible. The light wind felt good while we were cruising on the West Side Highway; however, I wasn't too happy with the disruption of my perfect hairstyle. The heat was at full blast as the fresh air was a bit cold with the top down.

We found an empty bench on the "sandless" Nyack Beach, facing the remarkable lights of the majestic Tappan Zee Bridge. We sat there in silence and admired all the beauty around us. The trees were still proudly displaying their greenest leaves while attentively eavesdropping on our quiet conversation. It felt different that night. I felt protected. I didn't have that tingling feeling in my knees, nor was my heart beating faster than usual, but I knew I wanted to get to know him more. I also realized that sometimes the exhilarating feeling of a high school crush could be highly misleading; therefore, I was willing to wait, get to know Jay and gradually feel the sparkling tingle in my tummy. At that point in my life, I was a single mother still trying to figure out motherhood. I thought maybe Jay could be the man I wanted in my life.

He was sweet, kind, gentle, and he wanted to uncover my essence. He was about 6'3" with a brown complexion. His slender frame made him appear taller than he was. He was funny and smiled a lot, just like me. We both were born in February, one year and five days apart. Our cosmic signs were the same, but our way of thinking couldn't have been more different. Jay adored me and treated me with respect. He tried to make me happy the best way he knew how. We were still in our early twenties and probably thought we knew everything about life. I was slowly learning how to love, and I gradually learned to trust him. I didn't have to guess his thoughts. He made it very clear that he wanted to be with me. I was more careful. I listened more, and I made sure I read the signs.

I remembered in college I subconsciously went out on dates with only light skinned and white men until I met Rafy and Michael. Perhaps I didn't appreciate my pretty brown skin then, so I sought men who didn't quite remind me of my darkness. I avoided all Haitian men because my infantile mind generalized a whole nation and put them inside a box. Jay was still struggling to put the pieces together in his life financially and emotionally. Although we were about the same age, I was years ahead of him in terms of financial stability. I had already owned a fully operational mortgage company, and the subprime mortgage industry was booming, and I still held my full-time job in the financial services industry. I was a long way ahead of my previously low salaried position.

Jay and I organically learned how to cope with the ups and downs of life, and we made our relationship work for a long time—that was until we decided to move in together. During the seven years we were together, I thought I understood the sacrifices required for a couple to stay together, but I soon discovered I still had a lot to learn about a relationship. Although we undoubtedly loved each other, I came to the conclusion that a strong connection between two individuals cannot be sustained only with love. Jay and I viewed life through different lenses. I was always pushing myself to do more because I did not want to become a victim of my past, and I certainly didn't want to be seen as merely a single mother. I craved success, even though I didn't even understand what success meant to me then.

I remember when I first decided to buy a house, Jay tried to convince me to continue to share a small two-bedroom apartment with my brother, until we were both ready to contribute financially toward my goal. Patience was never my strong suit; hence, I sped up the process without his consent. I figured since I had a daughter, I needed her to grow freely in her own environment, have her own bedroom, so I desperately wanted to create that reality for her. So, purchasing a home was a big goal that I wanted to cross off my list. I often visualized having my own house similar to a Manhattan penthouse layout, with modern furniture, glass doors, and marble countertops and my den overlooking the big city. I clearly saw an open space with minimal furniture. I could smell the baked cinnamon cookies, and I envisioned the fresh cut roses on the dining room table.

I was fully ready to purchase my home. Jay, on the other hand, was at a different place altogether. He was still living with his parents and was still trying to figure out his life. He had never lived on his own before meeting me; therefore, he did not have the same desire as I did. Our goals were not aligned. While I was always seeking more stability, he was still trying to find himself.

I confused his inability to provide financially as a lack of ambition. Jay was a black man working hard to make it in the corporate world. Shy of a few credits to complete his bachelor's degree in Architecture Engineering, Jay found that the jobs available in his field were scarce, and very few people were willing to hire a young black man without a four-year degree. I believed that it must have been trying for him to see me thriving financially, and psychologically, he was probably intimidated by my "success." I became somewhat the provider as I was slowly taking over his role as the man in the relationship. Now that I have had time to reflect on our relationship, he must have felt emasculated. In a way, I didn't allow Jay to be the man that I wholeheartedly knew that he could have been. I just took over his role. In my 20-something mind, I did believe that I never disrespected him; however, my actions proved otherwise.

I did not consult with him regarding my financial decisions; I simply told him what my thoughts were and took actions without involving him in the process. He must have suffered silently and felt dismissed and disrespected. We spent seven years together and engaged for a little over a year before we decided to part ways a few weeks before our wedding ceremony. When Jay and I broke up, I learned all about a broken heart. Jay was my best friend, my partner, my lover, and my "ex-future-husband."

When we broke up, his absence created a hole in my heart. My heart ached for a long time, and my first reaction was to fight for him, even though I knew we were not on the same wavelength, and had we had gotten married then, we would probably have been divorced within a year. I can now understand why Jay was hesitant to get married after being engaged for a year. He clearly wasn't ready, and he wasn't working. Perhaps, he didn't feel secure within the relationship, or maybe he didn't feel valued. Why couldn't I have understood his reasoning for wanting to postpone the wedding to a later date?

I had to convince myself that I needed to set him free. I had let go of him and the idea of marrying him. After a while, I noticed the pain had slowly subsided with mental peace, reflection, and eventually, I started creating new memories, and gradually the thought of being with Jay began to escape my everyday thoughts, and he became a distant memory. Jay's love was sweet, innocent, and sometimes unconditional. His gentle kisses were always reassuring, and I knew for sure he loved me with no hidden agenda. He showed me that I can be loved and I can learn to reciprocate love.

I thought Jay would have been in my life forever; however, I didn't understand the sacrifices that were required to keep a relationship together. I should have known to maintain my intimate relationship privately and not share every detail with my friends and family members. I should have talked to him as opposed to talking at him. I should have respected him enough to make him feel that his opinion mattered. I should have just loved him like Dany had loved me many years ago.

It has been many years since Jay and I broke up, and I decided not to keep in touch after one of our last conversations. It was always more natural for me to stay away. I knew staying in contact with Jay would be painful, and since I never liked the idea of hurting myself, I kept my distance. The more I stayed away, the easier it was for my heart to let go of him. I sometimes wondered where he was on his journey. Perhaps one day our thoughts will somehow interconnect, and we will find each other again. I allowed life to happen while I focused on becoming a better version of myself. When Jay and I parted ways, I also unintentionally distanced myself from my dearest friend, Teety, Jay's sister. The pain was too intense, and she always reminded me of him. I loved and cherished her many years of friendship, but I had to find a way to forget, move on, and find myself. I felt lost.

CHAPTER NINE

Toxicity of My So-Called Love

Over the years, I loved so deeply that my love had no boundaries. I loved intensely with unspoken expectations. I loved unselfishly and focused all my energy on my partner. I wanted my man to adore me the same way I displayed my affection toward him – intensely, passionately, and generously. I stayed in toxic relationships because I didn't want to believe that I deserved better. I walked away and came back time and time again, even after being broken emotionally, and abused verbally. I stayed when my partner didn't support my dreams, when my goals became irrelevant, and I stayed even when my partner chose not to include me in any of his future plans. I remained in a toxic relationship for so long that I started to believe I didn't matter without a man. I stayed because my self-esteem was brutally beaten.

I allowed men who did not care for me to occupy valuable space in my life. My primary food tank was utterly depleted, and I had no idea how to refuel it. I didn't realize that I had to love myself first before I could attract anyone to like me, and even love me. I couldn't give what I did not have. I desperately needed to learn to appreciate and love myself enough and allow positive energy to enter my life organically.

I reconnected with my Haitian roots when I met George, a beautiful dark chocolate skinned Haitian man with the whitest smile. He was tall, about 6'3" and had a muscular physique that had my mind wondering all sort of provocative thoughts. He was a sexy man. George and I spent hours on the phone talking about anything and everything. I often laughed a little more flirtatious during our conversations, and I started seeing the beauty of my brown skin through his eyes. I was drawn to him, especially when he told me a joke in Creole that I could immediately relate to, "Bel Ti Fi." Beautiful girl, that's how he called me every time we started a conversation. There was an undeniable connection between us. We spoke and understood the same dialect, although our love language was very different.

We talked about Haiti, our memories as children, and he promised to help me rediscover my homeland and its wonders. He often reminded me of the beauty of my culture, and I always welcomed the CDs from various Haitian artists that he had purchased for me. I had forgotten how beautiful and sensuous Haitian Kompa was, and George surely gave me a reminder every time he pulled me closer, and we danced to the distinct beat of combining musical instruments.

George also told me that he recently ended his engagement, but unfortunately, his ex-fiancé was pregnant, and he wanted to be present for his child. He assured me that they were not together. All I gathered from that conversation was a good and honest man who wanted to be there for his child and naïvely I was okay with that. The warning signs were not as clear to me then as they are now. Either that or I chose to ignore the bright neon warning signs that were unmistakably staring at me. I usually let myself get entangled in romance, especially when I received fresh cut flowers and a handwritten card. "You are one in a million. I am thankful for you," he wrote. I've always been a sucker for romance, and flowers had a way of temporarily robbing me of my better judgment. And receiving a greeting card from George profoundly touched my heart, especially in the modern age of the cold virtual world.

I spent countless hours on the phone talking to George, and slowly time spent with friends started to diminish. My usual after work Thursdays networking gradually stopped. Going to essential milestone events were abruptly interrupted if he couldn't accompany me. My decisions became dependent on his reactions, and if he wasn't pleased with any of my actions, I immediately stopped. I frankly did not understand the new layer of myself. I completely became submissive. George had a fascinating way of controlling me with only his words, and he lived 250 miles away from me!

The weekends didn't come fast enough with the anticipation of seeing him. I boarded the 5:50 AM Amtrak from Pennsylvania Station, on 34th Street to Union Station, Washington, D.C. The entire train ride took four hours and has cost me a few hundred dollars. Since I lived in the Hudson Valley area, I left my house at 3:45 in the morning to arrive in New York City on time, taking into consideration possible traffic. I parked my car for two days at a parking garage close to Penn Station and walked four blocks in the wee hours of the morning to reach my destination. I was always thankful that the city of the island of Manhattan was still full of people, no matter the time of the day. I thought the five-hour trip was a small sacrifice because I was excited to see my man. He greeted me with our signature kiss and those six words that made me rush into his arms – "you get more beautiful every week." Those words were worth every mile I took to get to George.

I met George during a frigid winter as the new year was about to start. His charm and charismatic personality got me hooked. For the first few months of our relationship, a strong friendship began to develop, and I longed to speak to him every day. He was attentive, intelligent, and he made me laugh. Underneath the charismatic charm, he was also an undercover bad boy who appeared to be genuine, and he quickly gained my trust. He told me enough truth to make me believe there was nothing hidden under the surface and was steadily getting access to my heart. He was amiable, and my friends adored him. One weekend I invited Anne to my house for dinner while George was in town. We sat on the patio. It was a beautiful star-lit night, and George dazzled my friend with his wit, charm, and attentiveness. "So, the two of you have been friends since college?" He smiled and caressed my hand. "I'm sure you both broke the hearts of nearly every guy on campus who you didn't give a second look at. Anne, you're beautiful, too." Even his laugh was charming. My friend laughed, and she took a sip of her lemonade drink.

George often made me question myself and my integrity. I wondered many times whether I was at fault by replaying a pity argument in my mind repeatedly, even though I knew there was no truth to his many accusations against me. One Saturday, we attended a barbecue in Brooklyn at his friend's house. While George was chatting with some people, I sat at a table as I did not know anyone there, and I did not want to talk with anyone knowing how George perceived friendliness as being flirtatious. A man approached me to casually say hello, perhaps because he noticed that I was sitting alone. I politely said hello and quickly told him that I was with someone as I pointed to George. He wished me a good evening and walked away. After we left the party, George was furious. "If you did not invite him, he would have never approached you," he said to me with total confidence. I did not have any more strength in me to defend myself, so I remained quiet as I did not want another fight that night.

George had total access to me and yet I only had limited access to him. I now understand that he was emotionally unavailable; however, he wanted me to be totally and completely available to him. I sometimes confused his possessiveness and jealousy with love. I often confided in him and was happy to have finally found someone with whom I could totally be open with, someone with whom I could share intimate details about my past. The more we talked, the more attached I became. I soon noticed that every time we had an argument, he would bring to light, intimate details that I had discussed in confidence with him, to hurt me. My trust in him started to diminish. I wasn't sure if I fell in love with George within the first few months of our relationship, but I knew with absolute certainty I was attached to him. After six months into the relationship, his snide and crude remarks became the norm with every argument.

The relationship became somewhat unbearable; yet every time I walked away, I always allowed him to step back into my life. The way I loved him was intense, and I felt like he was my kryptonite, and George had the power to lure me back in with merely his words. He showered me with enough affection to keep me around. He didn't have to show me that he had changed, although the disrespectful words would temporarily stop for perhaps a week or so, just to give me time to readjust.

I was still broken after all these years because I never dared to face my demons. My hidden thoughts kept on accumulating, and I was now unconsciously drowning in my toxic hidden reverie. My lack of appreciation for myself forced me to conform to George's mediocrity. I knew that our cosmic vibrations were not in sync and our energy didn't align, but I felt better about myself when there was a man in my life. The concept of spending time with myself once again became foreign to me. Every time I took a step forward, I felt like I was right back where I started. I still needed a man to make me feel whole.

I was excited to go to Haiti with George to celebrate my birthday. I was more comfortable with my decision because my sister, Patsy, worked for USAID in Haiti and had rented a beautiful house there. I knew I would stay at George's home, but the party would take place at my sister's house. I enjoyed planning my birthday party. I purchased the essentials that I needed in the States, especially excellent red wines, and cheese, and other nonperishable items. The thought of reconnecting with some of my friends who were still living in Haiti and the ones who had returned to their homeland made me more cheerful.

The hot sunshine welcomed us back home with a bright smile. We got out of Delta Airlines and walked toward the line for U.S. Citizens. I had parted ways with my Haitian citizenship as soon as I was able to. It felt strange being in my native country as a tourist, a stranger. I saw an older woman with multiple hats on her head, forming an ascending straight stairway. She made sure her luggage didn't exceed the weight limit of 50 lbs., so all twelve of her hats made it to her homeland with her, carefully piled up on top of her head. There were many travelers anxious to return home after many years. Some tourists appeared more at home than most natives, and there was me, curious to rediscover Haiti through different lenses, and seeing the beauty of my native land through George's eyes. Haiti had drastically changed, especially after the earthquake in January of 2012. The site of devastation was still visible even after three years. The blue tents covered the entire beautiful Champ de Mars that Dany and I used to escape to. The stunning national palace had collapsed. I was sad to see my country, but I was happy to be on vacation with my man, at his parents' house.

Since I've always been a planner, I had gotten a list of my special guests and sent an invitation to my friends and my sister's friends. Ever since I turned 30, I started enjoying celebrating my birthday every year. I also stopped focusing on the concept of age. In fact, I excluded my age as part of any conversation or discussion. I wanted to remain young forever, and this was my way of dealing with it. It wasn't that I wasn't proud of my age; I felt the more I focused on the fact that I was getting older, the older I would feel. So, I removed my age from the equation and focused more on my experiences. I was ecstatic to celebrate my birthday in Haiti and escape the cold winter of New York.

On a sunny Saturday afternoon at three o'clock, I was ready for my guests to arrive. I was happy to reconnect with Claudia from my former volleyball team and many other friends that I hadn't seen in many years. I also made new acquaintances with my sister's friends. My sister had introduced me to one of her male friends because he happened to work in the financial field as well. She thought we might have something in common to discuss. I spent a few minutes casually talking with him, while George was talking to other people that he had met at the party. I was happy, smiling, having a wonderful time, and drinking red wine. I was wearing a beautiful white dress, and at that moment I felt that everything was perfect. I must have been overly excited because I accidentally spilled red wine on my beautiful white dress. I immediately went inside to change with the only clothes that I had with me – shorts and a top borrowed from my sister. When I went back outside to rejoin my guests, George's disapproving look threw me off balance, and I couldn't continue to enjoy my birthday celebration.

Shortly after, he told me he was leaving. I could have stayed at my sister's house, but I chose to keep the peace and accompany him back to his parents' home.

That night was somewhat unusual. The thirty-minute ride to his home felt like an eternity, and his cold silence reminded me how inconsiderate he was, especially on my birthday. When we arrived at his parents' house, he told me that I had disrespected him.

"You always compromise my position as a man. You are so disrespectful." He spoke calmly, but with authority in his voice.

"Today is my birthday celebration. Are we really doing this?" I said furiously.

He came a little closer to me to hug me, and he started kissing me. I was mad and confused because I knew that I didn't do anything wrong, but I was still silently questioning myself, as his inquisition raised doubts in my mind. I didn't push him away. Perhaps sex could once again temporarily resolve our romantic misunderstandings, knowing that I was blatantly lying to myself. George often used sex as a seductive weapon, and I always welcomed it. Make-up sex was an exchange where I felt demoralized, and perhaps I thought I deserved to be punished. Was I being a bad girl for merely talking to my sister's friend? Was I flirtatious as he clearly reminded me while penetrating me harder and harder? Was I disrespectful to him as he kept on repeating with every stroke?

As he was ejaculating, he pushed a little harder, forcefully, and I felt a bit of pain and pleasure at the same time. I didn't cry, but I could feel my silent tears ready to burst. Was it sadness or fear that was crushing my soul? I had removed the makeup off my face, brushed my teeth, and laid right next to him, wondering why was I still in that relationship. When he pulled me toward him, held me a little closer, tighter, and I felt him deep inside of me, I forgot all the hurtful words, all the fights and for that moment I was his, and he was mine.

During my relationship with George, I have learned that outside influences of friends or family can also negatively impact a relationship. I had a habit of confiding in my friends when things were terrible. Mostly, I told them one side of the story. I didn't tell them how sweet George was when he felt a bit secure about himself, how we laughed so hard over stupid jokes, how he held me tight and his warmth made me feel protected, how when we danced in public, his eyes were fixated on me like I was the only woman in the world. He loved being around me, and he made me feel desirable.

We'd be strolling down DC in the Georgetown neighborhood, where some of our favorite restaurants were, and a song would play, its rhythm meeting us on the street. George would do an impromptu dance, sing the words, and translate. *Tu eres muy bonita.* These words were music to my ears. "You are so beautiful," he'd sing as he wrapped his arm around my waist, spinning me outward ever so gently and back to his arms. He followed it with a sensual kiss on my neck. His hopeful brown eyes met with mine, I melted, and my heart danced. I loved when George translated Spanish love songs for me. He was romantic, especially when his lack of confidence made a disappearance.

There was one particular night that is engraved in my memory. It was toward the end of April, his birthday, the fresh air and dry sky made our date night magical. I tapped him lightly on his knee, brushed my hand on his shoulder, and pulled his ear toward my mouth, "It's a surprise babe. I hope you like it." I whispered as he was adjusting his perfectly well-positioned cufflinks embellishing his light pink shirt and tailored navy-blue blazer. There was nothing to fix as he looked perfect. His nervousness was instead a sign of his uneasiness of not knowing our destination or rather not being in control. I could feel that he was tense as my knee lightly brushed against his outer thigh. I imagined all the unanswered questions going through his mind. I briefly looked up as the Uber driver was silently and steadily getting closer to our destination. I breathed a sigh of relief when George finally said, "Okay." It took weeks to plan this one evening, and I didn't want it to be spoiled. During the entire ride, I felt like I was between a calming sea and an angry ocean as the car was gliding toward the luxurious Mandarin hotel.

As we stepped into the beautifully decorated lobby, we walked toward the hostess who escorted us to CityZen, a fine dining American restaurant. George's smile indicated that he was pleased. The square tables were covered with a luxurious white cloth, accented with one small red candle that contrasted with the red carpeted floor. The plush beige leather chairs were inviting and welcoming. The dimmed circular chandeliers in the ceiling captured the romantic essence of the evening. We decided on the seven-course menu with wine pairing. With every bite and sip of wine, we became more relaxed and allowed the small detail of being the only black couple at CityZen that night to escape our minds. We laughed freely, gazed at each other's eyes, and his touch felt electrifying as he whispered, "Thank you, chérie, for a beautiful night." I knew deep down he cared about me in his own way. There are always two sides to a story, but sometimes it was easier to remember the bad times as my scars were probably still fresh, and my heart had not yet recovered from its wounds.

I allowed George back in my life so many times for over seven years because I tended to remember the good times. It was no longer an issue for him to continue to disrespect me. I suppose I became used to his familiar and subtle ways of disrespect. He knew I would somehow always take him back. I wasn't a challenge, and he no longer valued me as a woman. It didn't matter that I was there for him in any way possible. I became convenient. My misunderstood relationships were somewhat filled with confusion, chaos, or disrespect. I was responsible for the way I was treated. I allowed each and every one of these men to treat me a certain way. I showed them exactly how to handle me with constant disrespect. They treated me the same exact way I treated myself.

My intuition could have guided me had I allowed myself to listen to it. I have often rebelled against my internal instincts because I was weak, and I didn't understand that I held all the power. I didn't know that I controlled my destiny. Perhaps if I had taken a step back to see the signs, I would have walked away sooner. I should have looked closer into George's insecure eyes. They could have silently spoken the truth far more than his mouth.

It took me a while to let go of him, because I felt like I was walking away from love, and I was afraid to be alone. My emotions were raw, and I felt there was too much at stake if I gave up what was familiar. I did not fathom the thought of taking a new journey toward an unknown path. I have battled with my feelings because I was not ready to take action because I loved him. I had to learn to trust my instincts and muster the courage to make the right decision. My inner voice had always guided me into the right path when I allowed it.

Somehow, I found the courage to let go after many repeated cycles. The realization of allowing myself to be a doormat had sparked a fire within me, and I knew I needed to make gradual changes in my life if I wanted a real shot at joy and happiness. I had to shift my mind, and I became my own therapist. I was able to verbalize my feelings on paper, and I sometimes tried to reason with myself. First, I had to understand that I was enough, not to mention that I was a good woman. I began to learn to forgive and love myself. I started to like the person that was looking back at me in the mirror. I smiled, and I said to myself, *"you are beautiful"* a few times until the words started to sink into my mind. I complimented myself as often as I could, and I started believing that I was perfect with all my imperfections.

After seven years, I silently said goodbye to George. He left my house one Sunday afternoon after a pity fight. I decided this was the last time I would allow someone to have so much power over me. There were no final words. There was simply a lingering thought of walking away from him that finally came to fruition. I no longer had to explain myself. I just quietly removed myself from his life. Yes, I cried, and my heart was crushed, but I find that sometimes, silence can be much louder and more powerful than words.

Once I exited an unhealthy relationship, I used to have a negative view of all men. I was hurting myself by harboring such stereotypical thoughts. I understood that consuming these negative thoughts contributed to the attraction of the same type of men that I have always tried to avoid. I have learned that the law of attraction is real on so many levels. It has impacted me positively and negatively, depending on how I've swayed my thought process. For many years, I have attracted the same type of men because I've spent too much energy trying to avoid them. I needed to shift my mind, not necessarily to meet a different kind of man but to love and accept myself unconditionally. If I wanted to attract someone whole and confident, I couldn't stay broken myself. I started to take the time to work on myself. I built my self-confidence with words of affirmation and actions, and gradually, my new heightened energy allowed me to deal with issues positively. My mind simply needed a moment of peace and clarity, as my instincts were accurate most of the time.

I had to conclude that bringing order and discipline to my life required effort, determination, sometimes sacrifices and constant reminders. It was instead a challenging process for me, and my faith in many things was tested often. In the process of becoming a more confident woman, I've noticed that change of behavior requires time and self-discipline. I had to continually remind myself that anything worthwhile usually takes a while to accomplish. I had to relearn to value myself and my self-worth. I slowly started to treat myself a little kinder, gentler, and with the utmost respect. Yes, I faltered at times, but I found a way to remind myself that I was enough, I was beautiful, and I had to learn to love myself unconditionally before I could love others.

I had to show everyone, from men, to coworkers, friends, acquaintances and family members, how to treat me. During my process of discovery of self-love, I also uncovered the power of visualization and limitless possibilities that I could unlock with my thoughts. I started to replace my negative thoughts with positive and pleasant dreams. The moment I started visualizing what I wanted in my life, the more I noticed different positive things appearing from nowhere. I was a happier human being, and my tears were no longer near and ready to flow for every little turmoil in my life.

George had tried to once again contact me to wish me a happy birthday. I saw his number pop up on my mobile phone. The person I used to be would have pondered on the thought of picking up the phone, but I decided to let the phone cry loudly that day, as I reminded myself to change the distinctive ring tone that I had created for him. It's not like I stopped loving George; I simply disarmed him of the power that he had over me. I took a deep breath, and I turned my phone off, and wore a beautiful dress, checked myself in the long mirror in my bedroom, bent my hair forward to give it a bit more volume, and headed out to meet my friends for my birthday celebration.

CHAPTER TEN

My Dating Chronicles

The unavailability of men became a frequent topic. It created a myth that quickly appeared to be factual. There are indeed a lot of single, unmarried, and unwed women, especially in the Black community. I think our approach to dating is somewhat superficial, hence eliminating a lot of men from the dating pool. Also, I have noticed that a lot of women, including me, have slowly taken the role of the man in the relationship because of our robust jobs and careers. As money became the conversation topic of relationships, our attitudes sometimes left some men emasculated and out of sight.

It was about 8:30 in the evening on Tuesday, and I was happy to retire to my bed early. I had a long day. I took a long shower to remove all the anxiety and fear that usually accompanied my thoughts intermittently, and I released a deep breath because everything felt right at that moment. Comfortably in my bed, I grabbed my iPhone 7S version, and I briefly read the news headlines of the day. I was about to put the phone away when I remembered I downloaded Bumble a few days earlier for the fifth time. It is ironic how most of my friends usually say, "There are no men out there." I am regularly baffled by this statement.

The topic of the unavailability of men often left me uneasy. Does society want to infiltrate black women's minds with biased statistics, or was there any truth to that myth? Fortunately for me, I never believed that myth. In fact, I know there are a lot of men available, searching and hoping to find compatible women. Having dated online gave me a good idea of the pool of men in the marketplace. I am always puzzled when I hear women or even some statistics trying to convince black women there are no available men. It may indeed be more challenging to meet a perfect man or a potential husband. For me, it was much more challenging to identify what I needed in a man rather than finding one.

The conversation usually started with a simple hello through the virtual lens of cyberspace, a smile with a stranger at a New York City crowded lounge after a long day of work, or in the empty aisles of a supermarket. There were the nameless, the ones I knew from the first glance I wouldn't see again. Some remained strangers forever. There were those whom I crossed paths with again and pretended that I absolutely had no recollection of them. There were a few who didn't call me back because perhaps they could sense my lack of interest or maybe they just didn't feel a mental connection with me. I never pondered how they may have felt when I merely remained silent, yet I usually had a thousand unsubstantiated answers when they chose to stay away after a first date. There were a few last kisses, many unspoken goodbyes, many broken promises of 'see you later' and misinterpreted laughter.

There were those times that I wanted to walk away from a meal, but I stayed simply because I tried to force myself to be polite. They couldn't read me, and sometimes there were a few I couldn't read as well. There were those that I knew my heart was incapable of loving from the first glimpse. And there were those mysterious bad boys with mischievous smiles that I knew I should've stayed away from, but their irresistible charm drew me in. Some of those men were highly intelligent, successful, and available, but somehow, I convinced myself they were not a good match for me due to my then superficial qualities. There were a few whom I loved intensely, yet I knew that I had to walk away because they found a way to contribute to my self-degradation.

There were the ones who were infatuated and obsessed with me from the first glance of seeing me getting out of a yellow cab off Fifth Avenue in my 5" stilettos, because of their superficial views of me. There were the ones who got away. They had made their intentions known early in the courtship because they knew exactly what they wanted, but my heart let them get away because I wasn't quite ready for marriage.

My mind was stuck and confused. I could not really define what I was searching for in a man. It was not easy for me to identify what I needed. It was much easier for me to let go of suitable potential suitors because of a meaningless imperfection. It seemed as though I always had a mental checklist, and I was continuously checking and unchecking boxes, but the substance category was at the very bottom of my list. He was too short or smiled too broadly, he did not have table manners, or did not dress fashionable, or he arrived five minutes late, or just because the physical attraction was nonexistent. Sometimes my reason for dismissing a date was valid. There was one particular man who sucked on a toothpick throughout the date, even while walking on the street. The list was long and exhausting. I've realized I never grew out of that teenage mentality. I was always searching for something or someone to complement my life, but I had no idea what I was desperately seeking. Yet, in my mind, I was the sanest person in the world.

I met John through an online dating platform. After a few stimulating telephone conversations, he invited me for dinner. I initially canceled the first Saturday we were scheduled to meet because I was somewhat tired and it was rather cold, and I didn't feel like driving to NYC. He convinced me to meet him for brunch on Sunday instead, and since his voice was charming on the telephone, I agreed. My dates usually took place on a Saturday afternoon or in the middle of the workweek, usually after work. I made an exception to meet John on a Sunday afternoon for brunch at Sylvia's in Harlem. I arrived ahead of time as usual. The hostess guided me to my tiny square table while I waited for my date to come in the overcrowded cozy soul food restaurant.

The small restaurant was moderately decorated. The tables were covered with white tablecloths and accessorized with salt, pepper, ketchup, and hot sauce. The freshly made cornbread was delicious. As I took a bite, I glanced at the brunch menu. I ordered a Peach Tree Mimosa to settle my nervousness as my usual red wine was not available. The Sunday Brunch at Sylvia's must have been famous as there were no empty seats. I sipped on my mimosa, and I wondered why I never consumed alcoholic beverages in college. I always felt the watchful eye of my strict Haitian mother. I made light conversation with the female waitress who was too busy to really hear my vacuous joke about the weather, and I mentioned to her that I was waiting for someone. I ordered some snacks and waited for my semi-blind date to arrive.

I kept looking at the front door, so I could signal my date to my table once he arrived, in case my waitress was too busy attending to the other hungry customers. At precisely 1:30 PM, I noticed a man walking through the door. He was perhaps ten years older than the John I remembered in photographs, he was visibly shorter than him, and this man's stomach was much rounder than John's muscular abdomen as I recalled in one shirtless picture. I was thinking that he was running late and the man that walked through the door couldn't possibly be the charming John that I met online two weeks earlier.

I casually continued to browse the menu and impatiently waited for my actual date to arrive. I was about to signal the waitress assigned to my table to order some more cornbread when I saw her directing the older gentleman to my table. Did something happen to John? I thought it was actually sweet of him to send someone else to let me know that he couldn't make it.

"Hello, Bernadette. I am John," he said. He immediately recognized me, and at this point, I couldn't hide. I almost fell out of my chair! I wondered if he had read the disappointment on my face. Or was I that good at faking happiness? I smiled and simply said hello. I already knew that there was no connection within the first three seconds. I felt slightly annoyed when he asked me, "So how do you like it here in the States?" as if I had just moved to the United States. I felt like telling him that I have been here for over twenty-five years, and that question was no longer relevant. I politely smiled and said, "I love New York." I must have given him a dismissive look as he promptly changed the subject.

I purposely did not order anything else so I could speed up the process. Where was Anne when I needed her with the impromptu phone call? He was friendly, intelligent, and he tried his best to make small talk. I was screaming from the inside, *"LIAR."* Physical attraction and intelligence were my main two criteria of dating back then. I could have just told him that I had to leave with no explanation, but I was always concerned with hurting people's feelings. It didn't matter that this man did not represent himself truthfully online. I felt an obligation to stay and smiled while he was shamelessly enjoying his greasy fried fish. Was there something grossly wrong with me? I thought another date, another conversation, another meeting, and another "disconnection." I remained polite and made it through what seemed to be the most extended hour of my life. *"No. I will not call you,"* I wanted to scream when he asked me to call him when I reached home. I politely smiled and declined his offer to walk me to my car. There went another wasted afternoon.

I started to view dating as a chore, and it was no longer fun for me. I was so used to being in a long-term relationship, and it was getting difficult for me to get back on the dating market place every time a long-term relationship ended. Partying with friends became less frequent as I got older, and my friends were professional women who had busy lives. Some of them were married, had children, and had daily responsibilities to attend to. It was not as easy to get dressed and go out. When we finally went out to celebrate a milestone, most of them were on their mobile phones trying to stay connected with their family. A lounge or a bar was no longer a place to meet a potential mate, as mobile phones had replaced human interaction. And the men and women who did not have their phone out every single minute throughout the night were probably too shy to interact with one another. So online dating became the most comfortable and most convenient way to meet a man.

Then there was Jake. I met him at the Parlor on a Wednesday evening in June. I opted to drive that day and rushed through the heavy traffic of New York City as Jake made the reservation for 6:30. I parked my car at a parking garage, right next to the restaurant on Spring Street. A beautiful attendant walked me to the intimate bar, and I sat and waited for Jake. I opted out of my usual glass of red wine as I wasn't as nervous. I pensively looked at the fire pit in the middle of the entrance, and the romantic vibe of the place was soothing. The shiny dark wooden square tables were nicely dressed with folded white napkin cloths, and candles on the center of each table set a romantic mood.

The subtle light jazz playing in the background was precisely what I needed on a Wednesday evening after a long day of work. The Parlor was a private member social club known for fine casual dining. I already gave Jake a perfect 10 for selecting such an incredible place for a first date. The crowd was a mixture of the middle class and some affluent people of NYC. The mood was perfect. As I anticipated the moment, I heard a man in the distance say to someone else, "A beautiful woman is waiting for you at the bar." I looked toward the voice, and I saw him for the first time. He was walking toward me. I became increasingly nervous, and I thought that I should have gotten my glass of Malbec. He was wearing grey slacks and a cute striped blue shirt. His smile captured my attention immediately and right at that moment, I felt a tingling sensation in my stomach.

Jake was tall, slightly built, with a lighter than caramel complexion. His radiant smile had cured my slight migraine. I marveled at the beauty of this 43-year-old, well-kept specimen.

He was a handsome man. It helped that he was an Ivy League graduate and a successful black man! As he approached me, I smiled a happy smile, and he had awakened all my senses. He smelled good. Many pleasant thoughts were dancing in my head. I certainly didn't need the scheduled impromptu phone call from Anne. I didn't need to be rescued. He got my attention. We were escorted to our reserved table. We sat and looked at each other and smiled.

"You look amazingly beautiful." He said it with a combination of British, Ghanaian, and Brooklyn accent.

I thought he was a good-looking black man and well kept. "I am pleasantly surprised. You are very handsome." I complimented him. He smiled.

The waitress, dressed in a sophisticated little black dress, was attentive and polite. She gave us the menus. I looked at the tiny letters on the classic dinner menu, and I couldn't read anything. My poor eyesight wasn't cooperating, and once again reminded me that I was getting older. Why were the letters on a menu so small? I told the waitress that I would order the same thing as Jake, a salad of iceberg lettuce. How bad could this salad be? We talked about almost everything! I liked Jake, and I could tell that he echoed the same sentiments toward me.

He was truthful about being in a relationship that recently ended, having three children, and he also revealed some critical intimate details. I chose to consciously listen to everything that made him look good and ignored all the warning signs that potentially made him seem unappealing. That sensation in my stomach reminded me of a first high school crush, and I certainly didn't want to let go of that feeling. Jake slowly touched my hand tenderly, and he looked at me with his piercing brown eyes. I melted, and I felt a tingle through the walls of my vagina in anticipation of what was to come. Could Jake be the one? I prematurely thought about things that I dared escape my mind for fear of being judged. He slowly removed his hands from mine to make space for the food. My eyes smiled a flirtatious smile. I wasn't too hungry. The salad looked appetizing. I took a bite. Something tasted unnatural, a taste that I couldn't quickly detect. I asked him if he savored the same distinct flavor as I couldn't quite decipher what it was. He confirmed that he usually ordered this dish because of the unmistakable taste of the bacon. No! I was a vegetarian, and I didn't eat pork.

I happily blamed myself for not being able to read the tiny letters on the menu, not even with contact lenses. I guess next time I would need magnifying glasses, I thought to myself, and I laughed. Jake asked if I wanted to order something else; I declined. I didn't want the night to be over. I looked at my watch, and it was 10:30 PM and I had a 45-minute drive, and an early meeting the next day. Jake held my hand while he walked me to my car. "I had a great time. I hope to see more of you," he said as he smiled. Just after I said goodnight, he pulled me toward him and kissed me. I had these sudden urges inside that most would consider forbidden, provocative thoughts that somehow, I forbade myself to experience. Jake had awakened another side of me that had been forever dormant.

I could not wait to reconnect with him again. He suggested dinner in my town. He told me that he reserved the entire weekend for me. "I am available the entire weekend," he said. I was still formulating questions in my mind, and I didn't dare to ask them directly. Nevertheless, my heart was happy. At first, I thought it was too premature for Jake to know where I lived, but after much thought and consideration, I decided to let him meet me at my house. Jake convinced me to take one car to the restaurant. I happily obliged.

When his car pulled in front of my house, I was excited. I felt like a teenage girl in high school trying to escape her home from the back window. I got into his car, and we automatically kissed, like we had known each other for ages. I loved the smell of his cologne, and he looked sexy. He drove to the restaurant where he had reserved a table, and we talked like two old friends.

"I did not know about Ivy League schools when I was in high school. I made sure that my daughter did her research," I offered, reflecting on my early years and education.

"Mom was a professor, so I guess it came with the territory," he confided. It was easy to talk to him, and I did not feel like I was being judged. I allowed him to crack a dent in my wall.

Jake was open, and he seemed sincere. He told me he loved his ex-girlfriend. They were together for over 10 years. I wondered why they were never married, as they had three children together. He must have told me, but my eyes were so fixated on him, that the crucial details had escaped my mind. He confirmed he wasn't with her anymore and shared a personal story with me. From bits and pieces of the story, I immediately recognized who she was as I have seen her through my Facebook feed and on television talking about her story with passion. She appeared to be down to earth, and there was something I admired about her. She seemed to be smart and very confident, and she seemed happy behind the virtual lens, but I've realized there was something hidden behind her smile. The most beautiful, confident, and powerful women also cry in the dark, and they also have unanswered questions. From her story, I've gathered she loved her family and was very vocal about her personal and global humanitarian issues. I liked her, yet I didn't even know her. I didn't quite understand why my affection for Jake was so intense. Yes. I remembered. He told me he wasn't married by choice. I wondered how could any man not want to marry this incredible woman. And why did he walk away from her or had she walked away from him?

Everyone has a story, and there are always two sides. I couldn't help but wonder what Jake was looking for in a woman. He told me that she brought out the worst in him, and he did not like that. I didn't ask for details as I was afraid that I was not going to measure up to his expectations. What was he running away from? And why was I so scared to disappoint him? I flirtatiously danced to Sade playing in the background...in my mind. The glass of Malbec brought a new level of relaxation to my already non-calculated mind. I looked at him a little closer; his eyes sparkled with hope and perhaps admiration for me. He was more handsome than I remembered. I felt safe when he pulled me a little closer to him, and I allowed my mind and my energy to connect with him organically. The reflection of the dimmed lights in the ceiling made his light brown skin appear a shade darker.

I wanted Jake to make sweet passionate love to me the night he visited me. We sat on my white sofa and kissed passionately. I sat on him feeling all of him and kissed him so tenderly. He held me tight and pulled me closer. I could hear all the vibrations within my body, and yes, I wanted him deep inside of me, and I did not want the "good" girl syndrome to take over my brain. For God's sake, I was a grown woman, and I had no one to answer to but myself. For one night, I didn't want any deep thoughts. I just wanted to allow my desires to take over.

The vanilla-scented candle on the coffee table was burning slowly, and the heat level in my body was elevating fast. I fought with my thoughts as I didn't want any unpleasant ideas in my mind that night. I had never felt a sexual connection that was so intense. I was sure that I hadn't felt that way before. Then, of course, my thoughts had to ruin the party. The feeling of him not wanting to be married, and the idea of him walking away from that beautiful woman, and views of me not being enough for him, stopped me from proceeding further. I was mad at myself that night, but I felt that I reluctantly made the right decision. I may have inadvertently said goodbye to Jake that night.

A few months later, I remembered vacationing in Aruba with my daughter, and it had been a few months since I had spoken to Jake. After that night, we briefly talked over the phone or via text, but we didn't see much of each other. Maybe he was no longer interested in getting to know me, or perhaps he had decided to get back with the mother of his children. All my "maybe" questions were answered with an internal voice in my head. *"Dety, let it go."* It was as if my Nana was speaking to me.

Since I was now in a better position in my life emotionally, it was easier to let him go.

I was about to make a phone call using WhatsApp to contact my family in the States when I saw a message pop up on WhatsApp. "Hi B. Just reaching out to say hello. Perhaps we should go to Martha's Vineyard for a couple of days." It seemed like the wave of the ocean of the white sandy beach in Aruba became increasingly louder as I looked at the message for a while. I started typing a flirtatious and casual response, and I immediately used the backspace button and deleted it. I put the phone away in my beach bag and continued to enjoy my vacation with my daughter and my niece. As tempted as I was to see Jake again, I knew I deserved much more in my life. Jake was not ready to be in my life, so I let go of the idea of him before my heart got attached.

A year later, I was once again browsing through the thousands of pictures of men through the online dating marketplace, a different site, thinking how women can complain about a shortage of men when there are so many available men searching for one woman. Although ninety-five percent of my swipes were left, there were the five percent that appeared to be interesting. All I was searching for was for one man out of the millions available out there in the world waiting for that someone special. I usually took some time out of my now precious schedule to chat with the ones I was interested in, even for a minute before I decided to either see them in person or abruptly end the conversation.

I was visiting my family in New York. While I was browsing the many hopeful men waiting for their match, his online dating profile picture popped. I stopped, looked at his pictures, read his profile as if it was for the first time. He was still searching, still looking for someone, looking either for companionship or pleasure. He was still out there, searching, smiling, and maybe hoping just like me to find the perfect match. I smiled, admired his picture for a minute, and I swiped left. I said goodbye to Jake for the last time.

I was demanding and extremely particular about the men I have dated. I created a perfect partner in my head; a partner that didn't entirely exist. Perhaps I was imagining combining the different qualities of different men that I have dated and come up with the perfect man for me. Unrealistic as this may sound, this was my thinking for many years of my life, and at times, I had to keep reminding myself that there is no such thing as perfection. My expectations were clearly unrealistic, but I truly believed then that I would have met that perfect man. My search for perfection always geared me toward the men that were not quite suitable for me, but I still managed to find a few qualities that I liked in every man that I dated. There were also many things that I did not like. My partner and I were usually on a different spectrum. Sometimes, they were ready for a committed relationship, whereas I wasn't, and vice versa. But there was one particular man I never forgot because of his blunt honesty. His name was Julien.

I met him through a mutual friend. He was about 6'1" and had beautiful brown skin. He had a preppy style, which I admired. He looked sexy when he picked me up in his red Mini Cooper convertible for a short weekend getaway. He was the type of guy that would find the perfect place for a date, and always found a way to surprise me. Although he lived in Brooklyn and worked in NYC, he had a house in Pennsylvania. We had spent many weekends there. He often cooked for me and set the table with candle lights and one single rose. I really liked Julien, as he was attentive, romantic. He also was a good lover in bed. Julien was smart as well. He had received his MBA from Columbia University. We looked very sexy together. In my eyes, he was a keeper.

I spent a lot of time with him. He had spent an equal amount of time at my house as well, and would sometimes call out out sick from work to spend time with me. He loved being around me, and I welcomed it.

For the first seventeen months I dated Julien, he was my perfect man. I naturally assumed that Julien and I were committed because we were inseparable. I was making all sorts of plans in my mind, and it never occurred to me to ask Julien about the status of our relationship. Everything was perfect as I always pictured it. He even said that he loved me a few times, so I absolutely had nothing to worry about. I didn't take into consideration that I had never met his parents; but he did, however, attempt for me to meet his sisters, but they conveniently stepped out when we arrived at their house that weekend. I met all his close friends, and they all seemed to like me.

Julien was also attentive and often encouraged me to pursue my dreams. He believed in me and always tried to help me in any way he could. Julien was the one who inspired me to turn my basement in my house in New Hempstead into a beautiful studio apartment. He helped me grow as a person, and his actions proved that he cared for me deeply. There was one weekend that I did not hear from him. I found out afterward that he went on an overseas trip with his friends. I didn't understand why he couldn't merely tell me about the trip. When he returned from overseas, I spoke to him about his vacation, and for the first time, I took the opportunity to talk to him about the status of our relationship. He said to me, "Bern, I love you, but I cannot give you the white picket fence. I am not that family man.…...I want to be with you. I want things to stay the way they are. My ultimate goal is to make millions."

I realized I loved myself when I still felt a sense of peace when someone walked away from me. My stronger sense of self allowed me to attract more positive human beings to myself. I became more attuned to recognizing a broken man and understood that I was not the one responsible for putting the pieces back together for him. I also realized that it wasn't the responsibility of a man or anyone to make me happy. A lot of work has taken place within my mindset, and I now understand that I am enough. The broken woman within me had dissipated, and I was happy to now see happiness in everything. I noticed that I was always surrounded by beauty no matter where I was, so I felt that everything, no matter what it was, would be ok. I was no longer searching...

CHAPTER ELEVEN

Hunger to be Pleased and Unabashed

It was a pleasantly warm afternoon during the spring when I heard a vibrating noise coming from my bedroom. I was preparing dinner for my invited guests who were due to arrive at 4:00 PM. The table was set with candlelight, a small vase of white roses in the center, white square porcelain plates, and silverware; I wanted everything to be perfect. I always liked to entertain my closest friends and family, and on this particular day, I was preparing dinner for a few of my friends who were celebrating their birthday. I quickly browsed over the menu that I printed from Staples the day prior. Everything looked beautiful, and I was happy with all my preparations.

I was about to remove my unique ginger salmon with a hint of onions and fresh tomatoes from the oven when an irritating sound was getting louder. I removed my cooking gloves and ran upstairs to investigate the situation. Words failed me when I saw my five-year-old little girl place my vibrator on her forehead as if it were just another one of her toys. I stood frozen in silence, not quite sure how to react.

"This is mommy's toy, sweetie, now let me have it!" I finally garnered the courage to speak these words to Chrystie.

"No, mommy. I'm playing with it. I like playing with it," Chrystie protested as I took my toy and placed it safely in its box, promising myself to be more careful with my personal items.

"Give it back, mommy. Please?" Her little voice was determined.

"Why don't we get your new Bratz doll? You can bring it downstairs to have ice cream with you." I can't believe I was bargaining with my daughter to distract her from my vibrator.

I still don't know how she found it.

It has always been a battle for me to understand what made me comfortable and what I might genuinely enjoy when it came to intimate relations. I have always been timid when it comes to exploring my sexuality. My prudence stemmed from the fear of being judged by my partner; hence, there was always some sort of imposed limitation on my part. I often gravitated toward pleasing my partner as opposed to focusing on my own pleasure. Oddly enough, I have always found it hard to relax during intimate moments. For many years, I have put my partner's happiness and sexual satisfaction before my own. The lack of consideration for myself even manifested itself into my intimate life. I have often felt embattled with the inability to locate my G-spot.

I suppose I never really allowed myself to explore my body and all the power that it possesses. Truthfully, I was always hesitant to discuss intimacy with my friends, fearing that they may want me to express similar erotic stories of orgasmic fulfillment when I never could truly relate. I had yet to experience all of the sexual wonders that my friends had deliberately shared during our dinner conversations. I would laugh at all the lively discussions, thinking if only I could experience such joy during sexual intercourse. Now, don't get me wrong! Sex was enjoyable for me, but I've never experienced that euphoric feeling before I started connecting with my body, understanding myself a little bit more, and allowing my inner thoughts to quiet down.

"Stay right there, babe," I said to my lover as I felt myself about to experience what I thought was an orgasm. "Move your hips over just a little." For whatever reason, possibly a sudden onset of selective hearing, my lover instructed me to change my position. "But I'm almost there." I reluctantly complied, yet at the same time, I wanted to scream in my head. I knew at that moment, the chance of experiencing an orgasm had passed. *"Why on earth do you insist on changing positions so many times? I was so close."* My mind wondered. I guess for him, trying a different type of sexual position was satisfying…at least for him. All I wanted was to feel that tingly sensation that could make my legs weak. I wanted to feel that overwhelming explosion erupt throughout my body; to feel his warmth as his breathing becomes increasingly louder. All I wanted was to experience unadulterated pleasure. Perhaps he had already decided that we would switch positions five times not even taking into consideration that my body had tightened, that I held him a little closer, and that I wanted him to stay right there. My mind screamed, *"NO. I will not cum for you. I can't cum for you. You've just ruined it."* Another missed opportunity for a perfectly good orgasm.

I've always been fascinated by my friends' tales of their intimate moments; all the deliciously tantalizing tales of climaxing and orgasms. I would hang on with excitement to each articulated word, daydreaming about their descriptions of intense pleasure, as if they were reliving every single moment. As I sat there, diligently soaking in every word of the salacious details of my friends' sexual dalliances, I sat still wondering if I had ever experienced any of these erotic feelings… Honestly, I wasn't even sure how it felt to have a climax of sexual excitement. I assumed it was when I became tired during sexual intercourse, or when my body didn't want the intense pounding. Perhaps I was just a prude, incapable of exploring my sexual fantasies with my partner. Despite my astute attention to every detail of the described sexual exploits of my friends, I just couldn't comprehend engaging in such hedonistic coquetries, as described by my friends.

Although I've always been in long term relationships, I have often felt alone. Loneliness is not usually the physical act of being alone, but instead being with your partner physically, while mentally escaping to a more emotionally satisfying place. I wondered many times how could I possibly allow myself to be at peace while making love. My thoughts were always the most vigorous during sex. My mind just could not relax no matter how hard I tried. I wanted to experience the feeling that would render my friends speechless. Like the erotic renderings described by my closest friends, I desired a sexual encounter that would make my legs shake. I craved the feeling that would send my body into a shock of waves.

I realized I had placed too many restrictions on myself because I always wanted to appear to be "a good woman." As ridiculous as this may sound, this is precisely how I felt for many years. Why was it so important to me to be the quintessential good woman? I grew up in a culture and in a household where the subject of sex was a taboo. I was considered "a bad girl" if I were to voice my intimate preferences during sex. I grew up in a society where sexual pleasure was explicitly reserved for men. It appeared to me that sex was like a job, not to be enjoyed for mutual pleasure. Nevertheless, times have changed, and the period I grew up in was perhaps the last era of such backward views and opinions governing sex.

Being exposed to a different culture allowed me to act on my curiosity, and explore my body and learn that having an orgasm is not only a mutual pleasure but is actually healthy. While I cannot detail all of the biological underpinnings of an orgasm, I finally experienced it, and my body crashed for a couple of minutes. I felt a new form of mental and physical energy. My mind had a new level of clarity. I felt like a modern woman. Even if I couldn't exercise my inner wildness, I at least wanted to understand and experience the thing that made my friends deliriously happy. I realize now that I confused experiencing sexual freedom as being "a bad girl." I began to understand that women who were not concerned about what society thought were most satisfied. Men seem to appreciate a carefree woman, who owns her prerogative, mentally and physically.

I bravely walked the streets of New City; I skipped all the clothing stores, the excellent restaurants, and the healthy juice bars. I looked suspiciously guilty as I saw the flamboyant sign above the sex store. I wondered if some perverted man would be there to greet me. The thought of it made me cringe and almost change my mind. I took a step toward the store, pulled the door quickly, so no one would see me.

Of course, the door was locked, so I had to ring a bell! I wanted to run, but I stood there until I was buzzed in. There was a beautiful woman who appeared quite sophisticated at the counter and offered her assistance. I was shy as I explained that I wanted a vibrator. She showed me so many different vibrators that I became dizzy. I settled on a basic model, thanked her, and made my escape! I was so embarrassed as I placed my new toy at the bottom of my handbag, hoping that no one would ever see it. I realized that I've always made things more complicated than they should have been. I've stressed over the little things as opposed to seeing the bigger picture. Why was it so stressful for me just to purchase a sex toy? Why did I always feel so bound by the limitations that I imposed on myself? I sanctioned myself, and always thought someone or society was judging me; meanwhile, no one had me to think about...

My own limitations may have caused me to miss out on many opportunities; whether it was a sexual exploration or a missed promotion. It was ironic how many people have told me they were intimidated by me, and I always asked myself why. When I thought I had no power, I was usually holding all the cards, and still deep into the game. All I needed was a little self-love, self-assurance, and most importantly, I needed myself. The sex toys may have been purchased for one specific purpose, but in the process, I was liberated, and I was able to show my partner, without insulting his ego, how to please me.

I now know my sensitive spots, and I know what feels right, what's tolerable, and what's comfortable. Intimacy is not supposed to hurt or feel forced. I believe that it is necessary that both parties equally enjoy themselves. Over time, I have learned to just relax and enjoy the intense pleasure without the guilt. I learned to slowly please myself unabashedly while I let all the thoughts of frustration escape my mind. I finally had an orgasm that I imagined during intimate story time.

CHAPTER TWELVE

Friendships, Encounters & Experiences

It was supposed to be her day, and one of the happiest days of her life. It was March 24, Anne's 30th birthday celebration. The room was alive with her friends and family, ready to celebrate her special milestone. When she entered the room, she looked stunning and happy. I was delighted to see her smile. I remember her buying me my first stuffed animal, "Mr. Lion" after Jay and I parted ways. Her greeting cards always had words of encouragement and kept me afloat during my time of sorrow, and she made sure that *"I Will Survive"* became my theme song. She was always trying to help me mend my broken heart throughout my failed relationships. Anne loved life and tried her best to live it.

There was a period of her life where the light in her eyes had disappeared, and she couldn't let her happiness shine as she had met an undercover bad boy who wanted to control her life. I was happy when she was able to break away from that relationship. It took her a while to find herself again. When I saw her on the night of her birthday celebration, I knew that she had undoubtedly recovered from her complicated relationship because her eyes sparkled again, and I had the pleasure to once again see the happy, free-spirited 18-year-old girl that I had met in college. For a long time, she had lost her laughter and free spirit. I felt her pain like it was my own, but I was helpless. She needed to break away on her own time and in her own terms. It's ironic, I always wondered why she stayed in that toxic relationship for so long, but I finally understood when I was in a toxic relationship myself. She deserved all the happiness that came her way, and I was honored to celebrate her special birthday with her. The Soca music in the background made me forget all my worries. I allowed myself to escape my natural heavy mind and enjoyed that present moment, my dearest Anne's 30th birthday celebration.

Her boyfriend was there by her side that night admiring her beauty, and her free-spirited energy. She had met him a few years ago and became romantically involved two years earlier. The Soca music had stopped, and everyone was looking her way as her boyfriend got on one knee and proposed to her. I was so excited for her, and my heart smiled and cried at the same time. I was so happy for my best friend, but there was always someone, or some thought continually reminding me of my failures. I remember that night, a girl I used to know, took my hands and asked me, "Where is your ring?" Perhaps she didn't realize my engagement with Jay had ended. Maybe she was hurtful or malicious, or just perhaps she failed to remember that moment belonged to Anne. Words failed me that night. Anyway, it wasn't my night.

I looked at her with teary eyes, and I couldn't muster my pain, frustration, anger, the disappointment in myself. The sound of the music became intensely too loud, yet I forced myself to stay as I did not want to ruin the happy moment for my friend. It was a little over a year since I had broken off my engagement with Jay. I was happy for my best friend, but I was sad for that little girl in me still lost and searching for something unknown, even in her thirties.

Naturally, Anne asked me to be part of the bridal party as one of her bridesmaids. Jivie was her maid of honor. She had selected a few of her closest friends to celebrate her special day with her. This was the most painful thing my best friend could have asked me. I remembered every time we went to a salon to view bridesmaids' dresses, I felt like I was being poked with small needles all over my body. I felt the kind of pain you feel when you have a migraine that never goes away. My heart started to ache all over again and reminded me of what could have been. My wedding was supposed to happen a little over a year ago, and now I was just reliving the pain of my breakup. I should have been over Jay by now. At that moment I couldn't be happy for my friend, and I hated myself for feeling that way.

I became uninterested, and my participation in wedding salon visits grew infrequent. Anne loved a fairytale wedding, and she planned her wedding as such. I remember one day, she sent me a link to look at a bridal dress. The dress was stunning, and I felt some warm tears flowing down my cheeks. It was the day I realized that I couldn't continue to torture myself. I couldn't be my best friend's bridesmaid. It was too painful for me.

In my loaner Mercedes Benz convertible, I took a glimpse at this gorgeous bride standing on the step of a beautiful church in the Bronx, while I was looking for a parking spot. Anne was one of the most beautiful brides I have ever seen. The photographer was trying to capture her picture before her attendees arrived. I should have been there with her to reassure her that everything was going to be okay, although deep down, I had a feeling that she already knew. I should have been the one holding her beautiful long white train while she was trying to escape the many eyes that were fixated on her. I heard a loud horn behind me, alerting me that I was in the middle of the street gazing at my best friend.

And most importantly, I should have sat closer to her family and friends who were part of the wedding party. I selfishly kept myself away from the fear of reliving the pain that I experienced a year prior. All I could do was just smile. I attended my best friend Anne's wedding as a guest, not part of the wedding party. I knew this hurt my friend, a lot. It hurt me, too, and only added to the pain that I was already feeling from the reminder that my dream of being a bride a year ago was just that – a dream. She looked stunningly beautiful. Every detail was perfect. I hugged her, but I knew she was mad at me.

She wrote me a letter after the wedding detailing how disappointed and how hurt she was, and I finally told her how I felt. I wasn't sure why I wasn't frank with Anne about my feelings. Perhaps it was because I did not want her to think that I was jealous of her happiness. That was the farthest thing from the truth. I guess I was still holding on to my past and did not know how to let go of past relationships. I had a way of making things more complicated than they should be.

Had I talked to her then, she would have understood how I felt, and I would have been there for her special day. I felt like I have failed her as she was always there for me for every celebration in my life. Thankfully, real friends have a way of forgiving stupid mistakes. She knew my heart and knew how happy I was for her and how much I loved her. After all, she is the godmother of my princess, and she is the kind of friend who became my family. She helped me see life through joyous lenses even though she has had her own share of countless disappointments and emotional pains. She is the kind of girl who loves hard, and she is forever still my dearest Anne.

Kianna told me she was getting married two weeks before her wedding. She said verbatim, "What are you doing on the 19th of September?"

That was her way of inviting me to her wedding. She was one of my closest friends, my business partner, and was like a sister to me, and she never broke away from being extremely secretive. Kianna was my reality check. She reminded me that we all have flaws and that sometimes we have our own pains, own secrets, and personal issues. We hide things that are painful to us, and that is okay, too.

Through Kianna, I have learned that I didn't have to reveal every intimate detail of my life to people, and specific aspects of my life should remain private. There are no perfect humans, and our imperfections make the world a little bit more interesting. After my friend Kianna was married, she was faced with a painful realization of not being able to conceive a child, and that was something that her heart had desired for a long time. She wanted to be a mother. She desperately wanted to have a child with her husband. He was patient with her and understood that their options for being parents meant that Kianna would never become pregnant. I remember one day when Kianna called me in tears. "Why is this happening to me? All my life, any time I wanted something, my parents always told me to try harder. I always tried harder and eventually got the very thing I wanted. Why isn't that good enough this time? I can't work harder at getting pregnant because it's not going to happen." I listened and interjected only a few times. There really wasn't much that I could say that would make a difference. I could hear the disappointment and exasperation in her voice.

Again, I questioned God. Sometimes, I didn't understand his plans, even though my faith never faltered. Kianna was very religious, and she may have prayed for years for God to bless her with a little girl or little boy. I am sure at some point, she must have been mad at God for perhaps not listening to her many prayers on her scheduled time. Kianna suffered in silence. I know that she, at times, felt inadequate because she couldn't bear a child. I sometimes pleaded with God for her and wondered if God had perhaps too many requests at the same time and couldn't possibly grant them all. Little did I know that so many women were dealing with infertility issues, and they were hiding their pains from the world, just like my friend Kianna. I could imagine that on rare occasions, she had a love and hate relationship with God. She opened her heart to different possibilities and adopted two beautiful children, but I could still see the sadness in her eyes and the feeling of incompleteness, even after the adoption.

As I get older, I have learned to understand and accept my friends as they are, with all their imperfections. I've also learned that God surprises us with answered prayers amid those imperfect moments. Kianna couldn't even believe that carrying her own child was a possibility until she gave birth to a healthy little boy. She kept it a secret because she was scared, and she did not want to be robbed of the chance to go through this experience on her own. Kianna wanted to experience her pregnancy in her own terms. She wanted to feel every pain, discomfort, and most importantly, life inside her belly. She wanted to make sure this time it was real.

I wasn't mad at my friend for keeping such incredible news from me. I was rather disappointed. I felt sad that she didn't give me a chance to share that joy with her that I so desired for her so many years. But then again, Kianna is known for keeping secrets, and that's okay. She has always been there for me in every sense of the word. She is loyal, kind, stubborn, loving, supportive, and until this day, she is one of my closest friends.

As I become more mature and have acquired a little bit of wisdom, I have learned to accept people for who they are as long as whatever they are doing is not interfering with my life. I allow my friends to be who they are as individuals as long as there is a level of mutual respect and understanding.

The day I heard Ella's voice sobbing on the other end of the line, telling me she had breast cancer, was a heavy day. My emotions were mixed with fear and uncertainty. There were times I thought I had so many issues related to love, finances, relationships, and I didn't even realize that these issues could have been easily fixed. When I heard the word cancer, it was usually associated with life and death. It was black and white, and sometimes there were limited treatment options. I've seen my friend Ella going through the process of losing her breast, her hair, and the man she thought was the love of her life because he was too much of a coward to see her through her sickness. Ella was always a fighter, and her caring, sweet personality never changed – even when she was going through chemo. She still smiled through adversity and was as beautiful as ever. Her faith has been tested, her optimism may have been slightly shaken, yet her hope remained alive! I couldn't imagine then how I would have dealt with such a level of physical and emotional pain, but then again life has a particular way of waking me up every time I am a little bit too comfortable.

During my growth period, I had to learn when to let go of toxic attachments. There was this girl I used to know. Her name was Jade. We attended undergraduate school together. She used to call me at least ten times per day. The conversations were never productive. She always wanted to gossip about other people, and she demanded my attention. Her friendship became overwhelming, unbearable, and quite stressful, and she didn't respect any boundaries. Even though I was a friend to her for fifteen years, I had to cut her off. Her friendship was becoming toxic.

As I got older, my circle of friends became smaller. I had to end longtime friendships. Some people no longer had a place in my life, and when I felt the relationship was growing toxic, I had to stop it. Some friendships are meant to be forever. Some have an expiration date, and that's life. Along the way, I noticed that my circle of friends was becoming smaller, by a conscious choice. Once I understood the value of friendship, I started to appreciate the strong women in my tribe. My friends and I became a support system for each other, and slowly, my friends became my family.

CHAPTER THIRTEEN

I Kept Myself Shackled

Fear often had a way of impeding my ability to see beyond my limitations. I have allowed setbacks to stop me in my tracks many times. There were times I was just tired of trying to find my purpose of this life. There was a period in my life when I couldn't see my worth because the greatness within me had taken a backseat and allowed mediocrity to set in. Although deep down inside, I consciously knew what I had to do to succeed in the corporate environment, my thought process was somewhat demoralizing. I always wanted to have my own company. I tried to only use my corporate job to pay bills. Initially, I failed to understand I had a corporate responsibility to my current employer, and I had to push myself to do the best job that I could. I received this text years later from a former boss after I reached out to him to not only apologize but to thank him for wanting to push me beyond my abilities. *"From the first day, I knew you had great ability, and I expected great things, and I was not disappointed. You have been on a challenging journey, single working mom, and all the things that go with that, you overcame, and I am proud of you. This is not to say that the journey has ended, you still have more victories ahead, enjoy them but keep moving, remember discipline equals freedom."*

I was the girl who would arrive at the office very early in the morning and worked until dark. I kept my head down and worked hard. I was the girl who was willing to give advice to others on how to get promoted yet I sat there watching almost everyone I've trained climbing the corporate ladder while I patiently waited for my turn, and for my side business to grow. Deep down inside, I wasn't happy being in the same position for so many years, but because I was living in denial, I pretended this was okay with me. When my own business wasn't picking up as fast as I expected, I naturally assumed just being in the office early and leaving late would afford me a promotion. I waited year after year for upward mobility that never came to fruition. I have watched people whom I have trained over the years become my boss, and some have moved to different companies as top senior executives. I was disappointed in myself, and I grew demotivated and defensive. I mistakenly thought that promotion was about working hard, and that hopefully someone would notice me and promote me.

My definition of working hard was doing what's required. I never took into consideration that I had to present myself as a leader within my current position. I never understood that I had to show my bosses that I could lead by taking the initiative that would either aid in efficiency or the growth of the company. I did not get that promotion is about networking or knowing the primary stakeholders, not only within my region but also the global leaders that have an impact on the divisional organizational structure. After so many years had passed with no sign of promotion, I became frustrated with myself. I was always smart, I was sure that I was knowledgeable, and I believed that I was performing well. I didn't quite understand how I could possibly spend six long years at one place and never got promoted. When I graduated from college, I got a position at an import/export company as an office assistant. Within six months, I was promoted to the office manager. What went wrong? What was I doing differently? I was working at a top Fortune 500 company, and at some point, I enjoyed my job.

There were moments when I felt that I was at a crossroad, and I was stuck there. There were days that I dreaded going to the office. There were days I felt depressed and wanted to cry and have a pity party. There were many days where the thought of quitting came to mind, but I was too scared to walk away because of my many responsibilities. How could I have expected to be promoted when I've never given anyone any signals that I wanted to be a leader? I became a worker, not a critical thinker. Perhaps I had no clue how the corporate world worked. I had to somehow figure this out before I pulled all my hair out.

When I was a little girl growing up in Gommier, I felt that I could conquer the world. I was the top student in my class, I was considered smart, and people looked up to me. Somehow over the years, I felt that I have diverted from my path because I lost confidence in myself. Come to think of it, I never had a mentor to guide me. I was trying to figure things out on my own. Mentoring would have helped me along the way.

I decided to seek out other opportunities outside of my current firm because I knew that my bosses, along with my coworkers, had already formed an opinion of me. Sometimes it is difficult to change someone's view of you. It was too late for me to change the perception they had already formulated about me. I didn't present myself as someone who could lead; therefore, I couldn't have been promoted to lead a team within a top company. I found and paid a professional company to polish my résumé, and I was ready to seek a new opportunity. My strategy was different. Because I had a job, it was easier for me to be selective.

I polished my LinkedIn profile and was ready for a new beginning. Within a few days, I had an interview scheduled at a top company in Newark, NJ. I made sure I wore my best suit, and light makeup with conservative earrings and boarded the mid-afternoon train for my 3:00 pm interview.

I was interviewed by five people who didn't seem prepared for the interview. They asked me many questions that I thought were irrelevant; nevertheless, I pushed through and answered to the best of my abilities while I was already telling myself that I didn't want to work for this company. After I interviewed with five people within forty-five minutes, I was led to the office of the head of the department. At first glance, I realized she was a person that I aspired to be. She embodied a regal sense of confidence that could only be described by the overwhelming emotions that generated upon setting eyes on her. I knew this was not common. This was something I knew I needed. How could I embody so much confidence without even saying a word? This was my challenge to uncover.

Her name was Tiffany. Even though I knew I didn't want the job at that company, I was so thrilled to speak to her and ask her a few questions. I was curious to know a bit about her and whatever advice she could pass on. I asked her about what it would take to excel within her teams. She told me, "It's not about keeping your head down. You have to network." It seemed like she knew me, and she was telling me to get out of the way of my own success. I didn't network with anyone at work. I merely went to work, completed my daily tasks, and went home. I was pleased to have had an opportunity to talk to her. She had profoundly positively affected my life. I sent her a letter thanking her and told her that she had inspired me.

Fear had the power to impede my ability to see beyond my limitations. I have allowed setbacks to keep me shackled. I convinced myself that I was tired of trying. I forgot to ask myself what I wanted and how much I wanted it. The cold winter always found a way to mock my pain as I headed back toward my current office. I had a monthly mortgage note and a daughter to take care of. I wasn't about to walk away from a job without securing another. There were times that I wanted to stay in bed because I dreaded going to the office, but I knew that my job allowed me to live a somewhat comfortable life. I reluctantly boarded the train and headed to work. I started reading inspirational books during my morning train rides, and my eyes began to see the world more positively.

I no longer had the desire to blame the world, my managers, or my coworkers. It wasn't their fault I wasn't as successful as I wanted to be. I didn't take the proactive steps that were needed to reach the corporate ladder. I also realized that many jobs were available based on my skills, so I decided to actively take a step of faith and move from a very comfortable and safe environment to start a new beginning.

When I became a manager for a top company, I made it a point to mentor the people who were directly reporting to me. I felt that I had an obligation to show them the many ways to get to the top if that is what they desired. I have noticed that some people were stagnant and complacent, just like I used to be. I realized that I couldn't force someone to be ambitious. I could just make them aware of all the opportunities that were available to them within the company. I finally understood that I was the only one responsible for my career, and I had to manage it effectively. I now know that promotion is unlikely without camaraderie or networking. The after-work socialization with coworkers, especially with my bosses, paid off. Being involved in committees within my organization has transformed my career. I was visible, and these activities showed my interpersonal skills, effective communication, and passion for my work. One of the best moments of my life was when one of my directs told me, "I look up to you. Thank you for being the best manager I've ever had." I was filled with happy emotions.

Ironically, the only way for me to break from the shackles that were holding me back was to realize that I was the one holding the key. Once I took the initiative to make the changes that were needed to move forward in my career, the results were exactly what I wanted. I was moving up and becoming successful.

CHAPTER FOURTEEN

Changing Lanes

"I am going to miss this red hallway," I said to myself as I looked at the empty living room of my house, in New Hempstead, NY. I remember when Jay painted the red hallway leading to the bedrooms. At first, I didn't quite like it. Fifteen years later, I felt like the deep red symbolized so much more than a coat of paint. I had built a lot of memories there in fifteen years. This was the place I have seen my daughter grow up and becoming a woman. This was the place where I have had elaborate dinner parties with friends and family and had so much laughter. This is the very first place that I lived with someone I loved. This was the place of more sweet than painful memories. I looked at the empty space with the shiny hardwood floor, where my white sofa was strategically placed, and I reflected on all the good and bad memories. I have shed many tears, and I have also enjoyed some passionate lovemaking on that sofa. The beautiful mustard wall in the living room was bare of all the minimal paintings; only holes of the small nails were visible. I decided to leave the pretty long white curtains as I thought the new tenant would probably appreciate the cleanliness of the crisp white linen.

I remember the first time I laid eyes on that house that became my home. I had visited about ten houses that day, and none of them sparked any joy. Not sure whether it was the smell of old cooked foods that reminded me of the small 300-square foot room in Brooklyn or the uncleanliness that immediately gave me a warning that those houses were not for me. I remembered walking away disappointed from each of the ten homes I visited that day. The search was getting somewhat overwhelming for me, even though it was my very first day of looking at houses. Patience wasn't my best trait. Strangely enough, I was shopping for a home the same way I would have bought a beautiful dress for a special occasion. I did not like the concept of looking or searching for something for a very long time. Once I see something that my heart desires, I hold on to it. As my patience was running thin, and I wanted to attend to a few other tasks and errands that Saturday, my realtor, Daisy, suggested another house that wasn't on her original list. I figured that I should at least briefly look at the property.

The first time I walked in to the family room, the wooden panel on the walls were not impressive as it made the place look dark and smaller than it was, but when I walked into the living room and saw the open floor plan, similar to a penthouse in Manhattan, my eyes were beaming with joy. The clean bathroom and over-sized jacuzzi instantly made my decision for me. I acted purely on emotions. I never took a step back to thoroughly look at the small closet space, or the school district until after I signed the offer to purchase. Since my daughter was attending a private school, I felt that there was no need to ponder the school district. Little did I know that life would throw me some curveballs, and my daughter would have to indeed attend public school for two years. Acting on emotions never served me well. I had to learn to always take a step back and analyze the situation at hand before I fully committed to it.

I've needed to change lanes for a while. I have lived in New York for more than half of my life. I felt the need to walk away from what was familiar and start anew. My daughter, Chrystie, had just completed her undergraduate degree at Carnegie Mellon and was headed to Beijing with the help of a prestigious scholarship. I was happy, proud, and thankful. I thought it was the perfect time to leave New York and experience a new environment. When Chrystie was meticulously packing her two large suitcases to head to Beijing to complete her graduate degree on a fully funded fellowship, I knew it was the perfect time to say goodbye to my split-level home, in New Hempstead, NY. As much as I was going to miss all the elaborate parties and intimate dinners at my house with friends and family, I needed to find myself. I wanted to become a better version of myself. I am sure Chrystie has seen me cry a few times, but at the same time, I'd like to believe that she has seen more joy than sadness.

I must say that my internal thoughts were entirely in sync with my positive vibrations when I decided to move. After I dropped my daughter at the airport and hugged her tight to say goodbye, I was overpowered by overwhelming emotions. I did not want to cry, but I felt an involuntary tear on my cheek. I sure would miss her, but I knew she would be okay. A friend of mine decided to rent my house, and a job opportunity at an investment bank presented itself in Baltimore, Maryland. Without hesitation, I packed up my suitcase, made arrangements to rent my house, and got in my Toyota Highlander, and allowed the sound of Haitian and Zouk Music to lead me to my new destination.

I ended my longtime love affair with New York as my SUV slowly flowed into traffic on Interstate 95. The sunshine in July was quite refreshing, and I wondered whether all these people on the roads were heading southbound for a much-needed vacation on that Saturday, or whether they were heading home as I could not understand the traffic jam on such a big open highway. This was the very first time I would be in the city of Baltimore, although I have been to Maryland a few times before moving. Baltimore was never on my list of possible places to re-locate. In fact, I did not have a specific place in mind. I just envisioned a place with year-round beach weather, sunshine, and a pleasant, stable environment. Thankfully, my job interview took place at the New York City office, and via video conference. A trip to Baltimore was avoided at the time. Surprisingly, I did not have many convoluted thoughts about moving away. I was not anxious... I just felt happy. When I pulled up in the driveway of a beautiful, modest house in Baltimore, my heart rate intensified. I did it. I moved, and I wasn't scared.

My cousin, Ro, who lives in Baltimore, was kind enough to accom-modate me for two months. I never realized how much I was going to miss New York, my family, and all my friends. I was driving three and a half hours every weekend just to stay connected to my family and friends, or to get a glimpse of my old life. Deep down, I knew I would not look back, at least not for a long time. I needed this move to work. I always admired my younger sister, Patsy, who has traveled and worked in so many different countries. She never displayed fear or uncertainty. In fact, I felt like she was happiest when she was far away from every-thing familiar. I wasn't sure if she was running away, or she was thrilled being miles away from her family. I, on the other hand, have always been afraid to move away from familiarity. I liked the comfort and especially stability. Nevertheless, I am proud of myself to have taken such a big step.

Honestly, the only change that I usually welcome is directly re-lated to my professional life. Changes in my personal life made me uneasy; however, I realized that I needed to be uncomfortable to become the confident, independent, and humble person that was progressively bursting from within me. Perhaps, the inability to easily break away has kept me in many unhealthy friendships and relationships for longer than they should have lasted, although eventually I always managed to walk away from relationships that I deemed toxic. I had to find the courage and the ability to break the cycle of complacency, of fear, and I was proud of myself.

Baltimore is pale in comparison to New York; however, I started to discover its hidden charm after a year, when I moved to Mount Vernon. Transitioning to an apartment from a single-family home meant that I had to discard the unnecessary stuff and remove so much clutter from my life. I took the opportunity to not only eliminate physical clutter, but also the emotional confusion and baggage that still hindered me from freely moving to the beat of my drum. I was never attached to material things, so it was easier for me to part ways with so much unnecessary stuff that I had accumulated over the years. Sometimes I wasn't sure if the light depression that I briefly experienced a few times in my life contributed to the clutter, or whether the clutter had added to my anxiety. I realized I had to make a conscious effort to keep the things I really need and detach myself from the things that I thought I should hold on to. But clearly, I knew that they had served their purpose in my life.

I no longer had a fear of being alone, like my mother has been for so many years. Sometimes I wish she had married and had a companion to keep her company. I always wondered how she felt, and honestly, I felt guilty moving away, knowing that she lived alone. It was necessary for me to break away from my nest, as I needed to step back and take a good look at my world from the outside, with a sharper lens. With my younger sister, Patsy, living in South America, and Hody in New Jersey, we were far from our upbringing in Gommier, and sometimes the distance felt as equally far in my relationship with my mother. I don't know if it's because I was always searching for my most authentic self and anxiously looking for who I was becoming beyond the tested innocence of my childhood and teenage years. Perhaps there was a part of my mother in me that I never wanted to come to terms with.

CHAPTER FIFTEEN

Live in The Moment

His head almost hit the black microwave securely attached to the white wall, and he appeared much taller than I remembered. I sat on the mustard stool contrasting with the black marble highland and I smiled. The sweet sounds of *"You Got Me"* by The Roots and Erykah Badu brought a new layer of contentment to my heart. The aroma of the wild salmon was heavenly, and I imagined every bite would be delicious. I remembered how he used to cook for me when we were together. There was an art to the way he prepared food; he was meticulous about everything. I remembered I hardly cooked when we lived together as he was quite the chef. His five-star restaurant quality meals clearly displayed his love for the art of cooking. I loved eating his food. He slowly bounced his head to the sound of the music playing in the background. He seemed relaxed, happy, and at home. Fifteen years later, he was there, standing in my kitchen on Park Avenue in Baltimore. I was surprised to see him again, as I thought our past wouldn't have crossed paths once again, but life is full of surprises. He had his own life, and I surely had mine. We certainly have experienced many good and bad moments apart, and I am sure that life has either changed us for the better or perhaps has allowed us to see things differently.

Jay came to visit me with his sister, my friend Teety, whom I have reconnected with via LinkedIn. The visit was welcomed as I was at a point of my life where I craved friendship, love, or just to be in the company of people who knew me well, and who certainly cared about me. He was always a vegetarian, and years later, I became a vegetarian. He looked the same, hadn't changed much except he was more muscular than before. His tall, slim physique made him look younger than his 44 years of life. I smiled, and I contemplated the thought of rekindling our intimate relationship. I was single at the time. George and I had broken up over a year now. I took a step back to observe Jay's behavior as I was now a very different person than the 20-something-year-old woman he once knew. I was more mature, level-headed, and definitely more confident. I was more careful, and I learned to be happy whether or not I had a man in my life. I knew how to spend time with myself and enjoy every moment of it. In fact, time alone became a requirement for me. At that point in my life, I wanted to be with someone that could add value to my already enriched life, not someone that would merely fill a void. I was happier, secure, and comfortable in my own skin. I was no longer critical of myself as I found a way to embrace my faults and focus more on my positive attributes. I listened more than I talked.

We had a discussion about black women. Jay became visibly upset and started to express his views toward women of color in a condescending manner. He clearly was unsettled and wounded emotionally. He expressed his discontentment with black women. His generalization of black women being responsible for the issues that all black men were facing, left me baffled. Jay was dealing with his own pain and hurt as he had just gotten out of a destructive and abusive relationship. I understood that he wasn't quite over the breakup. I heard fear, anger, pain, and frustration in his voice. I wanted to hold him and try to make him feel better, but since my thought process was more logical, I refrained from doing so. I couldn't help but wonder what has the world done to the sweet and caring Jay that I used to know. His view of the world had become somewhat cynical, jaded and based on my assumption, he clearly no longer wanted to associate himself with a black woman on an intimate level, although his attention toward me told a different story. I was careful, and I listened attentively.

"Every black woman I meet is quick to tell me how she doesn't *need* a man, how her career is more important to her, or weekend getaways with her friends is more important." Jay was visibly frustrated, and though he didn't raise his voice, he did raise an interesting perspective that caused me to reflect on my life for a few minutes.

"I've even had a black woman to tell me that she can do for herself everything that a man could do for her. *Really?* That's what black women are thinking. Black men don't stand a chance." Jay held a glass of Cognac in his hand, attempting to take a sip, but allowing for his opinion to take priority instead. He continued to express his opinion, "Black women have a tendency of getting pregnant to trap a good guy. Many of my friends are going through that."

His way of thinking appeared somewhat juvenile, and any hope that was in my mind for us to rekindle our relationship quickly dissipated. There were moments throughout the whole weekend that took me back to the good times that Jay and I experienced while we were together. The time that I massaged his head, or when he gave me a shoulder massage, made me reminisce about the past and the possibilities of what could have been, and I also remembered the good times we enjoyed when we lived together. The brief, memorable moments spent with Jay that weekend in Baltimore made me realize what was still lacking in my life and what I needed, but I made sure I reminded myself that the Jay I knew had experienced his own growth as well. I immediately removed my emotions from the equation, smiled, and enjoyed a beautiful weekend with the people I love. At least now I knew I have acquired a new friend.

Every experience that happened in my life had taught me how to become a stronger person. Every relationship I've had contributed to something positive in my life, even though my heart suffered a great deal. I remembered when Jay and I broke up, two weeks before our wedding, I felt the urge to fight for him. After all, we were together for seven years. We shared a lot together. He helped me to walk away from him for good, and he had stopped me from fighting to restore our relationship. One day, I was on the phone pleading with him to come back home, and I used to cry often, and perhaps I sounded desperate on the phone. I never forgot the words that had allowed me to make a significant change in my life, "You are so weak." He said that on the other end of the line, but the sting was so sharp that he might as well have been standing in front of me. That day, I stopped calling him, and I stayed away.

A few years ago, I would have wondered if he thought I was still weak, but now I was in a different place. I was no longer searching. I was no longer looking at life through tinted glasses. I saw everything differently. I was different. I loved myself. I focused on the present moment, that weekend and the time I was spending with my friends. We ate savory foods, drank good wine, and celebrated the time we had together. I wanted to enjoy every second of my time. I've realized that the time seemed to be moving a little faster. At times, I heard the sounds of the milliseconds getting louder as the birthday celebrations became less frequent. The milestone birthday cards were no longer welcome. I didn't need to always remind myself of my age. Besides, what would be the purpose of it? I applaud women who embrace their age and proudly display it on social media. I have learned what may make one person happy, may make another person unhappy. I was living in a culture where divorce became a fashion statement and where people no longer fought for their relationships. It appeared that the first solution to resolving a simple misunderstanding within an intimate union was to walk away. Although certain things in society left me perplexed, I wanted to be present and live in the moment. I now was learning to take chances to make a meaningful connection with people I love and admire. I took the opportunity to savor every moment as if it was my last. I enjoyed the rest of the weekend with my friends, Jay and Teety. I no longer needed to over analyze everything, especially after my diagnosis.

It wasn't quite an ordinary weekend. It was Labor Day, and I took the opportunity to make the three-and-a-half-hour drive to New York to see my family. My daughter accompanied me that weekend. I realized how much she has grown and how poised and confident she was becoming. She had now received her master's degree from Tsinghua University in Beijing as a Schwarzman Scholar. I smiled with intense pride, and I thought to myself that I certainly did something right! I still remember the joy I experienced when I saw my daughter as the student speaker during her graduation ceremony at Carnegie Mellon. She was happy.

I looked at her, held her hand tight, and smiled. That day, I paid attention to the beauty of nature along the way. It was a sunny day with a clear sky and transparent bodies of water under the low and high bridges that reflected a sense of serenity and calmness. I wanted to feel warm and sweet hugs from my nephews, Hody's sons. They are always happy to see me and never want to let me leave any time I visit them. There is something special about my nephews' love; it is pure, safe, and for some odd reason, I feel protected when I am around my six and eleven-year-old nephews. They love me unconditionally.

There was also that unusual fifteen-day cough that wouldn't go away. It must have been allergies from the air conditioning. It had to be as my cough intensified every time I was in an air-conditioned environment. I thought I should go to urgent care the next day since there was one clinic not too far from my brother's home in Mahwah, NJ. I woke up early Sunday and decided to go instead to the emergency room at Good Samaritan Hospital in Suffern, New York. I drove around a few times as I could not initially find a parking spot. The thought of going back home crossed my mind as I was somewhat impatient, but the voice of reason took over. I quickly looked at my phone for any messages as I headed toward the big red "EMERGENCY ROOM" sign.

I approached the service desk where two women were seated. One was clearly mad about something insignificant and was venting, and the other was uninterested in her story. They clearly looked tired, and perhaps they wanted to be somewhere else. One of them forced a smile as I told them my reason for being there. Surprisingly, I heard someone call my name within minutes of registering. At least I would get my medication and would be on my way as soon as possible, or so I thought. She handed me a robe, took my vital signs, and disappeared. I never liked the smell of the hospital and undecorated white walls. I waited approximately two hours before the doctor arrived. We casually chatted about my two-week cough, and he confidently said that it could possibly be allergies, but he thought that it wasn't unreasonable to perform an x-ray.

I walked toward the x-ray room. I saw a woman who was screaming and couldn't stand still. I could see her physical pain through her watery eyes. I felt sorry for her. I was greeted by an x-ray technician and was asked to complete some paperwork. After that, my x-ray was performed. I wanted to rejoin my family and enjoy the rest of the weekend. I patiently waited for the results. It was cold, so I laid on my hospital bed to watch television under a warm blanket that a nurse had provided. I dozed off for a few minutes, and I suddenly woke up when my doctor entered the room. He looked at me with dark eyes and said, "I don't understand this, you look so healthy." I became curious and was wondering what he meant.

He took a deep breath and continued, "There is a mass in your lower lobe, and it appears to be cancer, but we are not 100% percent sure." I didn't believe him; therefore, my reaction was somewhat surprising to him. I said, "Well, there is no sense of worrying now until I get a biopsy done." He reluctantly agreed with me and made sure to express the urgency of my condition. He wanted me to wait for the radiologist who could give me a more detailed explanation. I just wanted to go home at this point. I waited for another hour because I wanted to get a copy of my x-ray. I was becoming increasingly impatient, and many thoughts started to bombard my mind. I walked to the nursing station to check myself out. They insisted I needed to see the radiologist. They called him, and we both walked back to my assigned hospital room.

He showed me the x-ray and explained to me that the type of mass I had was usually associated with CANCER. This was the last thing I heard. I became somewhat frightened as I often associated cancer with death. I called my brother, Hody, as I was unable to move for a while. I grew paralyzed with fear. His reassurance over the phone confirmed that the doctors must have made a mistake, and until I had a biopsy, I considered myself free of that deadly disease. I thanked the doctor, declined his many recommendations to consult with some New York physicians, took the copy of my scan from the nursing station, and checked myself out.

The seven-minute drive to my brother's house seemed incredibly long. I fought all the negative thoughts in my mind, and I refused to cry. I honestly started to believe that the doctor had made a mistake. I began to reflect on my life journey. How could I possibly have cancer when, for the most part, I was healthy? How could I have lung cancer when I never smoked a cigarette in my life? I couldn't comprehend it; therefore, I refused to accept my diagnosis. I arrived home and took comfort in my nephews' hugs. I shared the news with my family and reassured them that this complete misdiagnosis would be sorted out once I returned home to Maryland. I decided to continue to enjoy my long weekend even though the thought of cancer couldn't escape my mind.

I called my cousin, who is a radiologist at the University of Maryland. He referred me to his friend at the same hospital who specialized in "my condition." He took the liberty of making an appointment for me the following Tuesday. He also suggested that I meet with him so he could review my x-ray. After I spoke to my cousin, I made a decision not to approach my new condition with fear. I needed to remain level-headed and not panic, as this was the only rational way to deal with my demise. When my cousin reviewed my x-ray, he wasn't overly concerned as the mass appeared to be in the early stages. The only time I felt a single tear was when the biopsy confirmed it was cancer. At first, the thought of death briefly crossed my mind. The idea of losing my hair didn't scare me as much, as I felt that my hair could always grow back. That was until I started losing my hair. As I was reluctantly going through chemotherapy, my mind was temporarily in a darker place. My black hair contrasted with the white shower floor, and as it was coming out of my scalp forcefully, I couldn't hold my tears. I felt my hair sliding on my back and the water was washing away every strand of it. I didn't feel cleansed though. I felt imprisoned, chained, like someone was pulling me deep into a dirty hole. I heard myself crying loudly and uncontrollably. I knew it wasn't about losing my hair, but rather about losing control. One thing that I have realized is that being strong doesn't mean you don't cry, or doubt your faith sometimes, nor does it mean being temporarily in a bad place. I did wonder, "why me?" I imagined most people who have been diagnosed with cancer have questioned God. The thought of my older brother, Joe, who had died two years earlier, also crossed my mind.

I remember the last time I saw him at the hospital. I immediately thought about his life, his relationship with me, my other siblings, and my mother. He had finally migrated to the United States ten years after we arrived in New York. He was already married and had a child, so it was a bit more difficult for him to acquire a green card. Although my mother loved him in her own way, his life was much different than the rest of my siblings and me. He was considered the troublemaker of the family. He was kind and sweet and was always ready to lend a hand; however, he seemed like he was still rebelling, because maybe he never took time to deal with his internal uneasy thoughts.

He was a university professor in Haiti. Like some immigrants, when he migrated to the U.S., he surrounded himself with the wrong people; hence, he did not take the time to return to the university here to polish the skills that could afford him a better life. The type of work that came his way didn't match his intelligence. The people that he surrounded himself with were not a good influence. My brother lived with me for many years up until a month before he died. He returned to my mother's house because perhaps he felt that the end was near, as he had just received a heart transplant and was still having complications. He died in the wee hours of the morning at Good Samaritan Hospital.

When death came in the middle of the night, and cowardly took my 50-year-old brother, I understood how painful it was to lose someone close to my heart. It was a different kind of pain. It felt like I was surrounded by concrete walls, and they were closing in on me, and I couldn't escape. When I saw him for the last time, immobile on a hospital bed, I wanted to scream, but no sounds came out. My heart cried, ached, and bled at the same time.

Being diagnosed with cancer was not the worst thing that happened to me; however, dealing with unprofessional medical professionals was far worse. Having experienced and dealt with many things in my life, fear was no longer an option for me. I wanted to see my possibilities of staying alive, choose the best course of action that worked for me. Some medical professionals have unsuccessfully tried to infiltrate fear in my mind and wanted to rush me toward possible treatments that were not the best for me. I was far too strong, and with the help of my cousin, I found some excellent doctors and a superb oncologist who listened to my concerns and worked with me to come up with the best possible treatment that worked for me. The appointments with different doctors were scheduled very often, and it appeared that the doctors forgot I had a full-time job, and that I needed insurance from that job to pay for my medical care and treatments.

Adopting a healthy lifestyle was a necessary step for me when I was diagnosed with an autoimmune disease. Being a wellness coach in my spare time, it was easy for me to incorporate whole foods, superfoods, super greens, nuts, fruits, and vegetables into my diet. I hardly noticed any side effects with the healthy dose of the prescribed chemo drug I was taking once a day. When I started chemotherapy, the side effects were more apparent. I believe in the power of healthy foods, which helped with the healing process of my body. Every morning, I made it a point to consume my fruits and vegetables by way of juicing. I also researched some immune boosting vitamins. Every friend and family member had a different recommendation for me. I knew that their intentions were good; however, being bombarded with so much at one time can be overwhelming. Some of my friends just wanted to talk about cancer all the time, and they were somewhat careful with their words. I would often look at them with a bitter smile to let them know that they were acting crazy, and it was unbecoming of them. I was still the same person, yet they couldn't have a normal conversation with me. I would laugh and let them know that I am here, alive and well. God is not done with me yet! I am well, healthy, active, and thankful every day. I am grateful to have my friends, family, coworkers, and acquaintances in my corner.

When I started saying no to things and feelings that no longer served any purpose in my life, I started feeling stronger and acquired a sense of freedom and pride. I was able to quiet all the noise in my mind and allow a change that was profoundly significant to happen; hence, my internal and spiritual transformation began. There was a heightened aliveness that took place within me and made me question my actions and unkindness toward me. I was no longer seeking answers from my mother, my friends, or men. I had stopped seeking answers from my father long before he passed. I demanded answers from myself. I took a deep breath and decided that my constant tears of sadness would be no more, and my consciousness gradually walked away from my constant feeling of despair. My desire to embrace life and enjoy every moment slowly emerged as my new-found purpose.

I used to internalize and take to heart every emotion, everyday conversations, and every feeling. Now I simply breathe deeply, inhale, and release. My Nana was right. Everything is falling into place. I chose to appreciate the present moment, and I began to be grateful for the multitude of greatness that was happening in my life. I smiled widely as something profound has been revealed to me. My blessings had significantly surpassed my shortcomings, and I felt slightly guilty for not allowing myself to enjoy what was in front of me. I felt guilty for taking many things for granted. I now choose to live in the present moment and to love myself unconditionally.

Made in the
USA
Monee, IL